To:
Sonja

FAST
FRESH+
SIMPLE

Happy Cooking!

Hope Cohen

FAST FRESH+ SIMPLE

HOPE COHEN

Photographs by KRISTI SENAT

strawberryblonde press

Library of Congress Control Number:
2012942882
ISBN 978-0-9886147-0-3
Printed in China

Electronic version:
ISBN 978-0-9886147-1-0
To purchase an ebook visit
www.fastfreshandsimple.com

Photograpy by Kristi Senat
Edited by Andrew Schloss
Book and cover design by Denise Avayou
www.avayoudesign.com

Published by Strawberryblonde Press
Bryn Mawr, PA

ACKNOWLEDGEMENTS

Thank you to all of my family and friends
for your unwavering support as an idea became a reality

Mom for being you
Dad for teaching me a little bit about a lot of things
Lori for your brain and confidence
Cristy for being a true friend

Julien and Ella, the lights of my life, who are so full of love and respect,
always ready (and anxious) to taste-test anything and everything,
I am truly blessed

Bon Bon for being there and always lending a hand when needed
Iris for your faith and friendship
Richard for your confident encouragement, love and support

I would be remiss if I didn't thank my team,
without whom this book would not exist:

Andy Schloss for your voice and written word
Denise Avayou for your design (and awesome coffee)
Kristi Senat for your delicious photography
Lauren Markowitz for your smart kitchen assistance

CONTENTS

INTRODUCTION

For as long as I can remember, I have loved food and cooking. My earliest memories (I think I was in kindergarten) involve an Easy-Bake oven that my mother gave me. I was amazed at how I could stir the kid-size packages of cake mix with water, pop the resulting mixture in my toy oven, and magically a cake appeared! Cooking has been magic for me ever since.

My mother was a good cook, and as I recall the Sunday dinners of my childhood, I can't help but smile. During those critical years, the importance of family and sharing food around a table became a loving ritual, which has become central in my adult life. It is a big reason why I wrote this book, to help you and your family build soulful connections that will resonate for a lifetime. Even now, I can close my eyes and smell basil simmering in spaghetti sauce, or the garlicky aroma of salt-crusted roasts. I cherish those sensations and the memories they evoke — standing by my mom as she chopped, and tasted, and stirred, creating food memories for me and my family.

As a teen growing up in an inner city I couldn't help but absorb the world of exotic flavors enticing me from corner bodegas, delis, food stands and carts. I took a part-time job in a health food store that brought "organic" into my focus and taught me the benefits of connecting health and diet, with a heavy emphasis on vegetables. Meanwhile, in the midst of a life transition, my father became macrobiotic, and I dove into Japanese food and deeper into organics under his tutelage. We took Japanese cooking classes together experiencing new and unique ingredients that forever changed my palate.

Around the same time, I received a gift subscription to *Gourmet* magazine, which I devoured from cover to cover every month, traveling the world through its recipes. My family encouraged me to cook and I began to make them weekly dinners from *Gourmet*, but in no time I was venturing further, experimenting and creating dishes on my own.

I was fortunate to have the opportunity to travel at a young age to Italy and France, bringing reality to some of the dreams born in the pages of my well-worn copies of *Gourmet*. I absorbed all of the products I came across in every food market, at every restaurant, and in every specialty food shop. Each morsel I evaluated was filed away in the hard drive of my mind, available for future access when creating dishes in my own kitchen for my own family.

I took classes with chefs and respected home cooks in many of my travel destinations. I learned to make pasta at the side of an elderly Italian *nonna* in her dark farmhouse cucina. She spoke no English, and I spoke no Italian, but we had no problem communicating in the universal language of the kitchen. I learned to make soufflés in an old French chateau on a century-old stove, and how to cook with truffles in an ancient Italian "country house" that I later learned is code for "castle."

And all the time I read and imagined new dishes and flavor combinations. I discovered the ability to taste things in my mind and then accurately transform that flavorful thought into something delicious. When my children began preschool, I started to teach cooking classes from my home kitchen, and to write recipes based on my memory of what I had previously cooked. I started writing and collecting these recipes and used them in my culinary classes.

As a favor, a chef friend agreed to take me on as an apprentice in his kitchen once a week. That one day a week turned into a part-time job where I had the experience of working in a commercial restaurant kitchen, doing professionally the very things I loved the most. From one restaurant to the next, I continued to learn and expand my repertoire of dishes and knowledge of foods and cooking techniques. I was sure I had discovered the secret to happiness.

And then, through a chance encounter with a television producer at a dinner with friends, I landed a job hosting a cooking show that featured celebrated chefs cooking their specialties. This was literally a dream come true for me: half-hour sessions in a fabulously equipped kitchen, working side by side with talented chefs. I logged hundreds of hours over the years, working with nationally and internationally recognized chefs, bakers and sommeliers, learning new techniques and recipes and making new friends, which led to more opportunities to work in their kitchens and refine my craft further.

As a working single parent, it was extremely important that I nourish myself and my kids with healthy, great-tasting food. Often, I didn't know what I would be preparing for dinner until I went to the market at 4:00 in the afternoon. I wanted to cook foods that were not only quick and delicious tasting, but also beautiful on the plate. I realized that the recipes I prepared during the week were also the dishes I happily served while entertaining on the weekends. This is where and how the concept of *Fast, Fresh + Simple* was born.

I continue today to love food and cooking, wine and travel. Precious moments around my table form precious memories with loved ones, friends, family and extended family. My children are growing into young adults who share my passion for all things delicious and I cherish the moments we have shared and will continue to share in the kitchen and around our table.

I hope that with this collection of recipes, you are able to share my love for those memorable moments and discover that great food really can be *Fast, Fresh + Simple*.

Hope Cohen
May 2012

FAST
FRESH+
SIMPLE

COCKTAILS

CARLOS'S CARACOL CHÉ COQUITO

While vacationing in Rincón, Puerto Rico, I was introduced to this seductive, sweet and strong coconut/rum punch. Consider this creamy cocktail the Puerto Rican version of eggnog! Our congenial host and owner of the fantastic ocean-view villa where we stayed shared his recipe with me. I'm thrilled to be able to pass it along.

1   can (13½ fluid oz)
    coconut milk

1   can (14 fluid oz)
    sweetened condensed milk

1   can (5 fluid oz)
    evaporated milk

1   teaspoon ground cinnamon

1   teaspoon pure vanilla extract

4   egg yolks, lightly beaten

2   cups golden Puerto Rican rum

    Nutmeg, for garnish

MAKES 8 SERVINGS

Combine all ingredients in a blender. Blend well, refrigerate overnight and serve with freshly grated nutmeg. It will keep for several weeks refrigerated (highly unlikely that it will not be consumed).

BOURBON OLD FASHIONED

I never was a bourbon drinker, but recently became a convert, thanks to the latest surge in cocktail culture. Today's premium bourbons are beautifully balanced and richly flavored, thanks in part to America's newly found interest in small-batch producers. The wintery combination of orange, cherries, bitters and honey-rich bourbon is brilliant!

1 sugar cube

2 dashes of bitters

1 half-slice navel orange with the rind

1 jarred Italian Morello cherry (available at Trader Joe's and specialty stores)

1 ice cube

3 fluid ounces (about ⅓ cup) premium bourbon (I like Woodford Reserve)

MAKES 1 COCKTAIL

1. Place sugar cube and bitters in the bottom of a rocks glass and crush together with the back of a teaspoon or cocktail muddler until the sugar is dissolved.

2. Add the orange slice and cherry and crush together slightly.

3. Add ice and bourbon, stirring well to combine. Serve and enjoy.

LITCHI ROSE MARTINI

I adore the floral fruitiness of litchi, and combining it with rose and vodka could become habit forming!
Be sure to use good-quality vodka and serve very cold for a refreshing, floral treat.

3 ice cubes

6 fluid ounces (¾ cup)
   premium vodka

1 fluid ounce (2 tablespoons) rose
   syrup (available in Middle Eastern
   specialty stores) or alternately,
   a few drops of rose water
   (available at kitchen specialty
   stores)

1 fluid ounce (2 tablespoons) litchi
   syrup (from a can of litchi fruit)

1 canned litchi fruit, for garnish

MAKES 1 COCKTAIL

1. Put ice in a cocktail shaker or mixing glass. Add vodka, rose syrup, and litchi syrup. Shake your booty (and mixing glass) vigorously, until cocktail is icy and well chilled.

2. Strain into chilled martini glass and garnish with a litchi. Serve and enjoy.

GRAPEFRUIT GINGER MARGARITA

Grapefruit is an unexpected flavor combination with tequila, but it really works! I especially love the ginger/grapefruit combination. I developed this recipe after having a similar cocktail at the fabulous Four Seasons bar in Washington, DC.

3   ice cubes

1½ fluid ounces (3 tablespoons) reposado tequila

¾   fluid ounce (1½ tablespoons) ginger liqueur, such as Canton

2   fluid ounces (¼ cup) freshly squeezed pink grapefruit juice

1   fluid ounce (2 tablespoons) fresh lime juice

2   (¼-inch) slices fresh gingerroot

Grapefruit half-slice, garnish

MAKES 1 COCKTAIL

1. Put ice in a cocktail shaker or mixing glass. Add tequila, ginger liqueur, grapefruit juice, lime juice, and ginger, and shake well until extremely chilled.

2. Strain into chilled martini glass and garnish with grapefruit. Serve and enjoy.

PATRÓN BLACK CHERRY MARGARITA

Tequila is the ultimate feel-good liquor. This cocktail is my version of one that won first place in a competition where I was a judge, beating out more than 20 other contenders. All of the judges on my team agreed that the combination of flavors in this drink was *buena* (fine).

3 ice cubes

3 fluid ounces (about ⅓ cup) Patrón silver tequila

1 fluid ounce (2 tablespoons) orange liqueur, such as Cointreau

2 fluid ounces (¼ cup) fresh lime juice (approximately the juice of 1 lime)

½ cup pitted fresh black cherries, pureed with an immersion blender

Lime slice, for garnish

MAKES 1 COCKTAIL

1. Put ice in a cocktail shaker or mixing glass. Add tequila, orange liqueur, lime juice, and pureed cherries, and shake well.

2. Strain into chilled martini glasses and garnish with lime slice. Serve and enjoy.

PASSION FRUIT MOJITO

When the weather is warm and friends swing by for a BBQ or snacks on the terrace, serve these tropical mojitos, a fresh, fruity twist on the traditional lime/mint version. Passion fruit juice is available in most supermarkets in the juice or international aisle.

3 sprigs fresh mint

1 ice cube

2 fluid ounces (¼ cup) white rum

2 fluid ounces (¼ cup) passion fruit juice (Ceres or other brand)

2 fluid ounces (¼ cup) club soda

MAKES 1 COCKTAIL

1. Place 2 sprigs of mint in the bottom of an 8-ounce old fashioned glass and crush with the back of a teaspoon or cocktail muddler.

2. Add ice, rum, juice and soda. Stir well, garnish with remaining mint sprig. Serve and enjoy.

SUMMER SANGRIA FONTELLINA

Fontellina is a chic seaside Italian restaurant/beach club in Capri. The days there are spent lounging on the rocks in the sun, swimming in the inky blue Mediterranean Sea, eating divine food and drinking their famous sangria. La dolce vita starts and ends here!

1   bottle (750 ml) chilled crisp white wine (I like pinot grigio)

4   ripe peaches, peeled, pits removed, and each cut into 8 slices

4   ripe plums, peeled, pits removed, and each cut into 8 slices

4   ripe strawberries, washed, dried, green tops removed, sliced into quarters lengthwise

15   seedless white grapes, sliced in half lengthwise

2   mint sprigs

Ice for serving

MAKES 6 SERVINGS

Place all ingredients other than ice in a large glass pitcher; stir briefly and refrigerate for at least 2 hours or up to 4 hours. Stir well and serve over ice in wine glasses.

APPETIZERS, SNACKS + CONDIMENTS

ARTICHOKE BRUSCHETTA

Inspired by Carciofi alla Giudia, the glorious fried artichokes served throughout the Jewish quarter of Rome, these garlic-scented toasts are topped with pan-seared canned artichoke hearts (for convenience), drizzled with the best extra virgin olive oil you can afford, and confettied with freshly grated Parmigiano and chopped mint. Serve them with a rustic bottle of Italian sauvignon blanc and transport your taste buds to a rickety sidewalk table overlooking the Tiber.

1 can (14 oz) quartered artichoke hearts, drained well

4 tablespoon extra virgin olive oil

1 tablespoon finely chopped fresh mint leaves

1 small (about 8 oz) baguette, sliced into 18 (½-inch-thick) slices

1 garlic clove, peeled

Sea salt and freshly ground black pepper

½ cup freshly grated Parmigiano cheese, grated on a large-holed Microplane or grater

MAKES 18 TOASTS, 9 TO 10 SERVINGS

1. Preheat oven to 400°F.

2. Spread drained artichokes on a paper towels and blot to dry as thoroughly as possible.

3. Heat 2 tablespoons olive oil a large sauté pan (preferably cast iron) over medium-high heat until hot and shimmering, but not smoking. Carefully place the dried artichokes in the hot pan and season with salt and pepper. Allow artichokes to brown before turning, cooking until they are brown and crisp looking. Remove from the pan to the cutting board. When cool enough to touch, finely chop the artichoke hearts on a cutting board and transfer to a mixing bowl. Add the mint, reserving a small bit for garnish, and adjust the salt and pepper to taste. Stir to combine. *Note: The artichoke mixture can be prepared earlier in the day and reserved covered on the counter top, assembling the toasts when ready to serve.*

4. Place bread slices on a sheet pan lined with foil. Using a silicone brush, lightly brush bread with 1 tablespoon of the olive oil. Toast bread slices in the preheated oven until very lightly browned, about 5 minutes Allow bread to cool until you can lift a slice without burning your fingers and then rub each slice of bread with the peeled garlic clove.

5. Top each toast with some artichoke mixture (about 2 teaspoons), a drizzle of olive oil, and garnish with a big pinch of cheese (about 1 teaspoon) and a little pinch of chopped mint. Serve immediately.

RICOTTA TOASTS WITH THYME AND HONEY

Crisp toasted baguettes glow garlic. Ricotta relaxes in a cloud of cream. Grey-green specks of thyme blink under a golden sheen of honey—can you say mouthwatering?! These fresh cheese toasts are simple and quick to prepare for an impromptu gathering.

1 small (about 8 oz) baguette, sliced into 18 (½-inch-thick) slices

2 tablespoons extra virgin olive oil

1 garlic clove, peeled

2 cups good-quality ricotta, preferably homemade (page 30)

1 teaspoon fresh thyme leaves, finely chopped

Fleur de sel and freshly ground black pepper

6 tablespoons orange blossom honey, preferably in a squirt bottle

MAKES 18 TOASTS, 9 TO 10 SERVINGS

1. Preheat oven to 400°F, Place bread slices on a sheet pan lined with foil. Using a silicone brush, lightly brush bread with olive oil. Toast bread slices until lightly browned, about 5 minutes. Allow bread to cool until you can lift a slice without burning your fingers and then rub each slice of bread with the garlic clove.

2. Spread each garlic toast with a plop of ricotta cheese and sprinkle with chopped thyme. Season to taste with salt and black pepper. The toasts can be assembled to this point up to 2 hours ahead of time; cover loosely with plastic wrap.

3. Drizzle toasts with honey, sprinkle with a bit more fleur de sel. Place on a serving tray and serve immediately.

✳ Recipe for homemade ricotta on the next page ▶

HOMEMADE "RICOTTA"

Fresh ricotta cheese is the perfect vehicle for a myriad of dishes including but not limited to bruschetta, pastas, sandwiches etc., and while this isn't technically ricotta cheese, it is a fabulously fresh, creamy, simple homemade version that doesn't require the time and expertise of a cheese maker.

4 cups whole milk

3 tablespoons freshly squeezed lemon juice, strained of seeds and pulp

1 teaspoon sea salt

MAKES ABOUT 1 CUP

1. In a large heavy-bottomed pot (I use a Le Crueset enameled cast iron) bring the milk to a steamy simmer (about 180°F) over medium-high heat), stirring often with a wooden spoon to prevent burning.

2. Reduce the heat to low, add the lemon juice and continue to simmer and stir for about 2 minutes, or until you see small curds forming. Add salt, stir and remove from heat. Allow the mixture to stand for 10 minutes.

3. Carefully strain the mixture into a bowl with a large fine-mesh chinois or a strainer lined with a moistened double thickness of heavy-duty (fine) cheesecloth. Be sure to use ample amounts of cheesecloth so that you can tuck the ends under the edges of the strainer, so that the cheesecloth doesn't cave in while you are pouring the cheese mixture from the pot.

4. Cool to room temperature; the mixture will thicken as it cools. It may be refrigerated for several days (if you can restrain yourself from eating).

GOAT CHEESE WALNUT CHEESECAKES

This 21st century reinvention of June Cleaver's cheese ball is heady with herbs and fresh chèvre. Sophisticated and adorable, these miniature savory cheesecakes are the perfect hors d'oeuvre for a grown-ups-only cocktail party or served as an elegant appetizer on a tangle of vinaigrette-glazed greens when you want to make your best friend's other best friend jealous.

1 tablespoon melted unsalted butter, plus more for greasing muffin tins

½ cup fresh breadcrumbs

½ cup finely ground walnuts, plus additional nut halves for garnish

¾ teaspoon sea salt

¾ teaspoon freshly ground black pepper

4 ounces cream cheese, softened

5 ounces fresh chèvre (goat cheese)

1 large egg

1 tablespoon each chopped fresh chives, chopped fresh parsley, chopped fresh mint

1 clove garlic, peeled and finely minced with ¼ teaspoon sea salt

Spring greens and additional fresh chives, for garnish

MAKES 6 SERVINGS

1. Preheat oven to 350°F. Butter eighteen ⅛-cup mini muffin tins, (about 1 ¾ inches diameter and ¾ inch deep).

2. In a medium bowl, thoroughly combine breadcrumbs, ground walnuts, 1 tablespoon butter, ½ teaspoon of the salt, and ½ teaspoon pepper. Spoon a teaspoon of the walnut mixture into each cup and press down to form a bottom "crust."

3. With an electric mixer, beat the cream cheese until light and fluffy. Add goat cheese and beat until well combined. Add egg and beat until well combined. Add chives, parsley, mint and garlic and remaining ¼ teaspoons of salt and pepper. Divide the goat cheese mixture between the cups and smooth the tops. Set a walnut half on top of each cheesecake.

4. Bake until puffed and golden, about 15 minutes. Allow cheesecakes to cool for 5 minutes, then loosen with a knife, and lift carefully onto a serving platter, decorated with spring greens. Garnish with chives and serve warm. Cakes may be made several hours in advance and reheated in the tin before unmolding.

MINI POTATO PANCAKES, CRÈME FRAÎCHE AND SALMON ROE

This is my nana's latke recipe, probably passed down by her pogrom-fleeing Russian relatives. Forgive me, Nana. I've changed your down-to-earth dollop of sour cream into a heavenly pouf of crème fraîche, and I've crowned your humble potato pancake with some of the czar's caviar Oy! Choose salmon roe for a fabulous splash of orange-pink.

3   medium-large white or yellow potatoes, peeled and cut in 2-inch chunks

2   eggs, beaten

½   small yellow onion, peeled, trimmed, and cut in 2-inch chunks

    Sea salt and freshly ground black pepper

2   tablespoons matzo meal (available in the kosher section of supermarket)

    Vegetable or canola oil for sautéing

½   cup crème fraîche, purchased or homemade (page 174), for garnish

2   tablespoons chopped fresh chives

    Small jar (2 oz) salmon caviar (roe)

MAKES 12 PANCAKES, 4 TO 6 SERVINGS

1. Place peeled potatoes, eggs, onion, salt and pepper in food processor container. Process with steel blade until mushy and relatively smooth. Add the matzo meal and blend until just combined. Taste for seasoning, adding more salt or pepper, if needed.

2. Heat enough oil to coat the bottom of a large nonstick sauté pan over medium-high heat until hot, but not smoking.

3. Spoon heaping soup-spoonfuls of the potato mixture into miniature pancakes in the hot oil. Sauté until well browned, about 4 minutes, flip and brown on second side. Drain on a paper towel–lined dish. Can be kept warm or reheated on a rack set on a sheet pan in a 350°F oven for up to 20 minutes.

4. Mix crème fraîche with chives and salt to taste. Garnish pancakes with a small dollop of crème fraîche topped with a bit of caviar and serve immediately.

MINIATURE ASIAN CHICKEN MEATBALLS

I know meatballs are done to death, but when I entertain, I want to serve a good assortment of bite-size nibbles, and these miniature meatballs are so popular that I have to squelch my need to be a cutting edge entertainment doyenne and get down to the task of serving truly delicious food. That's really what a party is all about.

1 pound ground chicken breast meat

1 egg white, beaten just enough to loosen

1 can (8 oz) sliced water chestnuts, rinsed and drained

3 scallions, roots and dark greens trimmed, chopped

1 garlic clove, peeled and minced

1 teaspoon grated peeled gingerroot

1 teaspoon minced fresh jalapeño chile, without seeds

2 tablespoons mirin (sweet rice wine)

1 tablespoons tamari or soy sauce

Juice of ½ lime

1¼ teaspoons sea salt

1 cup panko (Japanese) breadcrumbs

2 tablespoons chopped fresh cilantro, plus more for garnish

2 teaspoons vegetable or canola oil

Kekap manis (sweet soy sauce), for garnish

MAKES 16 MEATBALLS, 4 SERVINGS

1. Preheat oven to 400°F.

2. Put chicken and egg white in the work bowl of a food processor and pulse until combined.

3. Put water chestnuts, scallions, garlic, ginger, jalapeño, mirin, tamari, lime juice and salt in the work bowl of a food processor and pulse until finely chopped. Add chicken, panko, and cilantro. Process briefly, just until everything is combined. Form mixture into miniature meatballs with your hands (mixture will be very moist) and place on an oiled sheet pan.

4. Bake until meatballs are firm and flecked with brown.

5. Put on a serving platter, drizzle with sweet soy sauce and garnish with more cilantro. Serve with decorative toothpicks.

MICROPLANE

The Microplane grater, originally named "rasp" and traditionally used in woodworking, has become an indispensible tool in the kitchen. The ergonomic handles and assorted blade sizes effortlessly shave and shred strands of cheese, citrus zest, spices, chocolate, garlic, vegetables and more. From the finest, small sized blade perfect for the most delicate tasks such as grating garlic or gingerroot to the larger, coarser blade perfect for grating vegetables into slaws, you will find yourself reaching for your Microplane time and time again.

SHRIMP AND DATES WRAPPED IN BACON

Sweet, savory, and salty sensations embrace and swirl. These pop-in-your-mouth morsels are a dance party across the tongue. They are equally at home served on picks as an hors d'oeuvre with cocktails, or on a tangled bed of baby greens as a sophisticated first course for your next dinner party. If you are preparing them for cocktails use medium shrimp, if for a first course, opt for jumbo.

2 dozen jumbo (16-20 count) shrimp, peeled and cleaned

2 garlic cloves, smashed, peeled and finely minced

½ teaspoon sea salt

Freshly ground black pepper

½ cup extra virgin olive oil

½ teaspoon ground cumin

1 tablespoon sherry vinegar

1 tablespoon finely chopped flat-leaf parsley

1 dozen strips good-quality bacon

2 dozen small, soft, medjool dates, pitted

MAKES 24 SHRIMP, 6 SERVINGS

1. Preheat oven to 375°F.

2. In a medium mixing bowl toss shrimp, garlic, salt, pepper, oil, cumin, vinegar and parsley. Mix well and set aside on the counter.

3. Cook the bacon over medium heat until approximately half cooked, still translucent and pliable, not crisp, about 5 minutes. Drain bacon on paper towels and cool. Cut each piece of bacon in half, the long way.

4. To wrap the shrimp, take a date and nestle into the curve of a shrimp. Wrap the shrimp and date together with a piece of bacon. Secure all the elements with a toothpick or small wooden skewer and place on a sheet pan. Repeat with remaining shrimp, dates, and bacon.

5. Roast the bacon-wrapped shrimp and dates until the bacon is crispy and the shrimp are just firm, 15 to 20 minutes. Blot with paper towels and serve immediately.

SCALLOP CEVICHE WITH ORANGE, MANGO AND MINT

Scallops make the most luscious ceviche (pronounced seh/vee/cheh), the bracingly fresh, almost raw marinated seafood slivers of Mexico and South America. But scallops are often adulterated, so look for those that are wild caught and unsoaked (see below). Not only is this delicate dish full of flavor and refreshing, but because it "cooks" without heat it just the thing when it's too hot to turn on a stove.

Juice of 1 lime

Juice of 1 juice orange

1 tablespoon finely minced scallion

½ jalapeño chile, stem and seeds removed, minced

3 large mint leaves, torn

Fleur de sel

6 large diver sea scallops, tough side muscles removed

¼ cup finely diced mango flesh

1 tablespoon, finely chopped cilantro

MAKES 4 SERVINGS

1. Combine lime juice, orange juice, scallion, jalapeño, mint leaves and fleur de sel to taste in a medium glass mixing bowl.

2. Slice each scallop horizontally into 4 even disks, about ¼ inch thick. Add scallops to citrus mixture ensuring that slices are completely submerged. Refrigerate until the scallops are opaque but still supple, about 2 hours.

3. Remove scallops from marinating liquid, reserving liquid. Arrange scallops on individual serving plates and garnish with some of the marinating liquid to moisten. Sprinkle with fleur de sel to taste. Garnish with diced mango and cilantro and serve immediately.

DIVER SCALLOPS

Scallops are frequently plumped (soaked) prior to selling for visual appeal and moisture retention. Recipes often call for scallops to be browned to contribute texture and flavor. However, scallops that have been plumped resist browning. During pan-searing, soaked scallops release so much moisture so quickly that surface browning is impossible. Unplumped scallops are sold as "diver scallops," "dry scallops" or "day boat scallops."

CANDIED BACON

These sugar-coated, caramelized, crunchy, salty, fatty, sweet strips of decadence are so addictive they probably should be illegal, as my son, Julien, has become addicted. Crumble them with goat cheese over a salad, or stack them on a bruschetta with some melted Fontina, or serve them with fried eggs. That is if there's anything left after you're done sneaking your share right off the counter.

12 strips thick-cut applewood-smoked bacon

Freshly ground black pepper

3 tablespoons dark brown sugar

MAKES 6 SERVINGS

1. Heat a flat griddle or large heavy sauté pan on medium heat. Sauté bacon, turning often, until golden brown on both sides, but still pliable, about 7 minutes.

2. Sprinkle bacon with pepper and sugar, as evenly as possible, turning to coat both sides, and continue to cook, watching carefully as it will brown quickly once the sugar is added. When bacon is brown and crispy, remove to paper towels and drain.

BLACK BEAN DIP

Black beans have glossy ebony skins that turn into warm mahogany when pureed into this fragrant citrus-laced dip that sparks and soothes with bits of jalapeño and cilantro. Make this dip a day or two ahead of your party and bring to room temperature prior to serving.

2 tablespoons extra virgin olive oil, plus additional for drizzling

1 small red onion, peeled and finely diced

1 small red bell pepper, stemmed, seeded and finely diced

1 small or medium (to taste) jalapeño chile, stemmed, seeded, and minced

1 garlic clove, smashed, peeled and chopped or pressed

1 teaspoon ground cumin

2 cans (15 oz each) black beans, drained and rinsed

Juice of 2 limes

1 tablespoon sherry vinegar

2 teaspoon sea salt, more or less to taste

2 to 3 tablespoons cold water

2 tablespoons chopped fresh cilantro

MAKES 6 SERVINGS

1. Heat olive oil in a nonstick sauté pan over medium-high heat for 30 seconds. Sauté onion, pepper and chile until onion is translucent, about 4 minutes. Add garlic and cumin, stirring until aromatic, about 30 seconds.

2. Transfer sautéed vegetables to the work bowl of a food processor fitted with the steel blade. Add the black beans, lime juice, sherry vinegar and salt. Process until smooth, adjusting seasoning to taste. Thin with water as needed.

3. Transfer to a bowl, drizzle with additional olive oil and garnish with cilantro. Serve warm or at room temperature, with tortilla chips and/or crudités.

LEMON HUMMUS

Hummus, the Middle Eastern chick pea meze, has as many flavor permutations as there are taste buds. My daughter, Ella, loves lots of lemon and garlic (reflected in this recipe), but really the recipe can be customized in endless ways. Remember that hummus becomes thicker as it sits, especially in the refrigerator. Serve it close to room temperature with crudités or pita toasts.

2   cans (19 oz each) chick peas (garbanzo beans), rinsed and drained

¼   cup extra virgin olive oil, plus more for garnish

2   garlic cloves, peeled and chopped or pressed

    Juice of 2 lemons

1   tablespoon tahini (sesame seed paste)

    Sea salt and freshly ground black pepper

    Water to thin consistency, if needed

    Sprinkle of ground cumin seed

MAKES 6 SERVINGS

1. Put the beans, olive oil, garlic, lemon juice, tahini, and salt and pepper to taste in the work bowl of a food processor fitted with a steel blade. Process for 60 to 90 seconds, until smooth. Add cold water to thin to desired consistency, if needed. It should be the consistency of mayonnaise.

2. Garnish with a drizzle of additional olive oil and a sprinkle of ground cumin. Serve with pita bread, pita toasts and/or crudités.

TZATZIKI (CUCUMBER YOGURT DIP)

Available in most every taverna in Greece, this piquant yogurt/cucumber dip is traditionally served as a meze-style appetizer plate with freshly grilled pita bread, but often left on the table throughout the entire meal as a condiment for grilled meats and fish. The flavor of any tzatziki is much improved by using long slender English cucumbers, rather than the slicing cucumbers that are squatter and thicker with tough dark green skin and large seeds. English cukes, which are usually wrapped in plastic rather than being coated in wax, have tiny seeds and are often sold as "seedless" or "burpless." They are sweeter and less bitter than slicing cucumbers.

1   English cucumber, peeled and halved lengthwise

4   cups plain Greek-style yogurt

1   large garlic clove, minced to a paste with salt

    Juice of 2 lemons

1   teaspoon salt

    Extra virgin olive oil, for garnish

1   tablespoon chopped flat-leaf parsley, for garnish

MAKES 1 QUART, 12 SERVINGS

1. Scrape the seed core from the cucumber halves by running a spoon down their length. Grate the halves into a bowl using the coarse teeth of a shredder or the shredding disk of a food processor.

2. Mix the yogurt, garlic, lemon juice, and salt in a mixing bowl until well combined. Drain cucumber of any juices and stir into yogurt mixture.

3. Transfer to a shallow serving bowl, drizzle with olive oil and garnish with parsley. Serve with toasted pita or use as a garnish for grilled or roasted meats and fish. May be made up to 24 hours ahead and refrigerated.

SMOKED SALMON SPREAD WITH DILL AND CAPERS

Scottish smoked salmon, redolent with fumes of oak smoke and a lingering zing of sea salt, longs for a buffer. This super fast and simple spread has fresh dill and capers, which when combined with cream cheese and slathered on crisp toast zip across the palate in perfect balance.

2   packages (8 oz each) cream cheese, room temperature

1   tablespoon minced red onion

2   tablespoon finely chopped fresh dill, plus additional sprigs for garnish

2   tablespoons small capers, drained

    Juice of ½ lemon

1   pound smoked Scottish salmon, chopped

    Toast points or crackers

1   small jar (2 oz) salmon caviar (roe), for garnish

MAKES 18 SERVINGS

1. Combine cream cheese, onion, dill, capers, and lemon juice in the work bowl of a food processor fitted with a steel blade. Using the pulse button, process until the ingredients are fully combined but still chunky, scraping down the sides as needed.

2. Add the chopped salmon and pulse with the cream cheese mixture just until combined.

3. To serve spread mixture onto toasts or crackers and garnish with salmon caviar and fresh dill sprigs.

TOMATILLO AVOCADO DIP

Back in the culinary dark ages of the 1990s when Nuevo Latino was still nuevo, the James Beard award-winning chef Guillermo Pernot and I worked together. He developed a recipe for Tomatillo Avocado Gazpacho, which inspired me to develop this fresher-than-fresh version of guacamole, its richness enlightened with the clean lemony tang of tomatillos.

6   tomatillos, husked, stemmed, and rinsed

2   ripe Hass avocados, quartered, pitted and peeled

1   cup loosely packed cilantro leaves, washed well and dried

1   tablespoon minced onion

   Juice of 2 limes

½   medium jalapeño chile (or more to taste), stemmed, seeded and chopped

⅓   cup sour cream

   Sea salt and freshly ground black pepper

   Raw vegetables (crudités) or chips

MAKES 6 SERVINGS

1. Cut the tomatillos and avocados in eighths. Put in the work bowl of a food processor fitted with a steel blade. Add cilantro, onion, lime juice, and jalapeño. Process until smooth, scraping down the sides as needed. Add sour cream, and pulse to combine. Season with salt and pepper to taste.

2. Transfer dip to a bowl. Serve with crudités and/or corn chips.

RÉMOULADE SAUCE AND DIP

This sauce is the perfect foil for crispy, sweet and succulent crab cakes (page 139). With that said, any fried fish, shellfish or shrimp cocktail can benefit from being dipped in this creamy, lemon-packed sauce. I am not a lover of most commercially-made mayonnaise. I prefer homemade, but if I must used jarred, I only use Hellman's real mayonnaise in this sauce.

1   cup homemade or purchased mayonnaise, preferably Hellman's

1   teaspoon finely chopped capers

1   teaspoon finely chopped cornichons or sour pickle

1   teaspoon finely chopped shallot

½   garlic clove, minced to a paste

½   teaspoon smooth Dijon mustard

Juice of 1 lemon

½   teaspoon Old Bay seasoning

1   teaspoon minced fresh parsley

1   teaspoon minced chives

Sea salt and freshly ground black pepper

MAKES ABOUT 1 CUP, 6 SERVINGS

Combine all ingredients well in a bowl. Chill covered for at least 2 hours. Can be prepared up to 48 hours in advance and kept in an airtight container until ready to use.

MANGO SALSA

The meaty flesh of ripe mango, saturated with natural sugars, and the perfume of the tropics joins the traditional salsa amigo-trio (tomato, onion and chile) to transport your flavor-drenched taste buds south of many borders. Equally at home on a chip or on top of a piece of grilled chicken, meat, fish or seafood, this versatile condiment/salsa/sauce should be a mainstay in your kitchen.

1   large ripe mango
    (about 1 ¼ pounds), peeled and
    cut in ¼-inch dice (about 2 cups)

3   plum tomatoes, stem-end
    removed, cut in ¼-inch dice

1   yellow or orange bell pepper,
    seeded, stemmed, and diced

1   small garlic clove, minced

2   tablespoons finely diced red
    onion (rinsed well in a strainer
    under cold running water
    and drained; see page 64)

½ to 1 jalapeño or serrano chile,
    stemmed, seeded and minced

2   tablespoons finely chopped
    cilantro leaves

1   tablespoon extra virgin olive oil
    Juice of 1 lime
    Sea salt and freshly ground
    black pepper

MAKES 3 CUPS, 8 SERVINGS

1. Toss diced mango, tomatoes, pepper, garlic, red onion, chile, and cilantro in a serving bowl.

2. Add the olive oil, lime juice, and salt and pepper to taste; toss to coat. Serve at room temperature with tortilla chips, plantain chips or as an accompaniment to grilled chicken, meat or fish. Refrigerate any leftovers for up to 1 day; bring to room temperature before serving.

DICING A MANGO

Peel the skin from the mango with a vegetable peeler or paring knife. Cut a thin slice from the thick end of the mango to create a flat surface for the mango to stand on. Stand the mango on the cut end and cut the sides off the center pit, curving the knife around the pit. Slice each half lengthwise into ¼-inch-thick slices. Cut the slices into ¼-inch-thick strips and cut the strips into ¼-inch cubes.

OSO SWEET ONION JAM

I developed this flavor-packed recipe for OSO Sweet brand onions, a deliciously sweet onion variety from California that has a very short season, only 5 weeks a year. If you can't find OSO brand, another reduced-pungency onion can be substituted. Note that so-called sweet varieties of onion do not have more sugar than standard yellow onions, they are just lower in volatile oils and therefore are less pungent and taste sweeter. Serve with grilled meats and chicken, as a condiment on a cheese plate and/or on sandwiches.

2 tablespoons butter

6 large OSO sweet onions (or other sweet variety)

Sea salt and freshly ground black pepper

¼ cup dark brown sugar

¼ cup granulated sugar

¼ cup sherry vinegar

MAKES ABOUT 1 CUP, 8 SERVINGS

1. Melt butter in a large frying pan over medium heat. Add the onions, salt and lots of pepper. Sauté until lightly caramelized (a uniform golden color), stirring often, about 45 minutes.

2. Stir in brown and granulated sugars and cook until onions are deeply caramelized (dark brown in color), 10 to 15 minutes more.

3. Add the vinegar and simmer until the liquid is reduced to a syrup, about 5 minutes. Add more salt and pepper to taste; cool to room temperature before serving. Store in a refrigerator in a closed container for up to 1 week.

RASPBERRY CRANBERRY CONSERVE

Think of this as cranberry sauce elevated to a raspberry level. Four-ingredients-easy (Ok, technically it's seven ingredients, but two are water and salt, and one is optional), this is a fabulously fast holiday (or everyday) condiment. Serve it with roasted turkey, pork or chicken, or slathered on a roast beef sandwich w/ havarti cheese.

8   ounces fresh cranberries, washed, and stems removed

¼   cup light brown sugar

½   cup granulated white sugar

½   cup water

Pinch of sea salt

2   cups fresh raspberries

1   tablespoon Chambord raspberry liqueur (optional)

MAKES ABOUT 3 CUPS, 12 SERVINGS

1. Mix cranberries, brown sugar, white sugar, water, and salt in a medium saucepan. Bring to a simmer over medium heat until the cranberries pop, about 5 minutes. Stir often to keep the mixture from boiling over; don't be concerned with the amount of foam.

2. Add the raspberries and simmer until everything is saucy consistency, about 5 minutes, stirring frequently. Turn off heat and stir in liqueur (if using). Conserve will gel from the natural pectin in the berries as it cools. Refrigerate and serve chilled or at room temperature. The sauce may be made several days ahead of time.

SOUP + SALAD

GREEN PEA SOUP PUREED WITH MINT

Bright emerald green and bursting with mint, this soup is simple and like a breath of fresh spring air. I am usually a stickler for using fresh vegetables, but when it comes to peas, I go for frozen most of the time. Green peas are highly perishable, losing a substantial amount of their nutrients and sugars within 24 hours of harvesting. This rapid deterioration is apparent whenever you look at the starchy, bland peas available in the produce section of most markets. These several-day-old peas can't compare with their frozen brethren that are blanched and frozen the day they are picked. You can taste and see the difference. Serve this soup warm on a chilly night or icy cold as a warm weather lunch.

1   teaspoon vegetable oil

2   scallions, trimmed and chopped

1   bag (9 oz) frozen baby peas

6   fresh mint leaves, chopped, plus tiny leaves for garnish

4   cups water

    Sea salt and freshly ground black pepper

3   tablespoons crème fraîche, purchased or homemade (page 174), for garnish

MAKES 4 SERVINGS

1. Heat oil in a heavy medium saucepan over medium heat. Add scallions and sauté until translucent, about 1 minute. Add peas, chopped mint, water, and salt and pepper to taste. Bring to a simmer and cook until peas are cooked through and still bright green, about 5 minutes. Remove from heat and cool for 5 minutes.

2. Pour into a blender, and blend carefully, allowing steam to escape (see note), stirring and scraping blender container as necessary, until ingredients are well pureed. Add additional water to thin the soup to desired consistency. Taste for seasoning, adding additional salt and pepper to taste. Serve immediately or allow to cool, refrigerate and serve chilled the next day. Note the soup may need additional thinning if served cold. Garnish each serving of soup with a dollop of crème fraîche, seasoned to taste with salt, and tiny mint leaves.

✳ NOTE: Be extra careful when blending hot ingredients in a blender to allow steam to escape by slightly moving lid to a side position or removing the center plastic part of the lid and covering with a towel so the ingredients don't splatter. Neglecting this step can cause a hot explosion.

ROASTED BUTTERNUT SQUASH SOUP

Roasting squash caramelizes its natural sugars, bringing out its rich savory qualities. Paired with the tartness of apple and the aromatics of onion and garlic, this soup rings with sweet and savory notes. Healthful and flavorful, it is easily converted to a vegetarian dish by substituting water or vegetable broth for chicken broth. Serve it with a salad, wine and some great bread, and you've got the perfect light dinner.

1   large or 2 small butternut squash, peeled, seeded and cut into large chunks

3   tablespoons extra virgin olive oil

Sea salt and freshly ground black pepper

1   sweet onion, such as Vidalia, peeled and chopped

2   celery ribs, chopped

3   garlic cloves, peeled and smashed

1   tart apple, such as Granny Smith, peeled, seeded, and coarsely chopped

1   sprig fresh sage

3   sprigs fresh thyme

6   cups chicken broth

MAKES 6 SERVINGS

1. Preheat oven to 375°F. Toss the squash chunks with 2 tablespoons of the oil on a sheet pan, season with salt and pepper and roast until lightly browned and tender when pierced with a fork, about 45 minutes.

2. While squash is roasting, heat the remaining 1 tablespoon oil in a large soup pot over medium-high heat. Add the onion, celery, garlic, apple, sage and thyme and sauté until the produce is just starting to soften, about 4 minutes. Season liberally with salt and pepper.

3. When the squash is done roasting, add to the soup pot along with the broth. Heat to a simmer and cook for 20 minutes, until all of the vegetables are very tender. Remove herb sprigs.

4. Carefully strain vegetables from liquid, reserving liquid. Puree vegetables in a food processor or blender, or with an immersion blender. Add some of the strained stock to thin, if necessary. Stir the pureed vegetables into the strained stock. Adjust seasoning and reheat before serving if needed.

CARROT SOUP WITH WARM SPICES

Close your eyes and take a whiff. The intoxicating fragrance of cardamom, ginger and cinnamon swirl around the natural sweetness of carrots, making this delicious pureed soup a delight for all the senses.

2 tablespoons unsalted butter

6 large carrots (as fresh as possible, preferably with greens still attached), greens trimmed, peeled, and cut in 2-inch chunks

1 leek, washed well and sliced thin

1 teaspoon peeled and minced gingerroot

½ teaspoon ground cardamom

Scant sprinkle of ground cinnamon

Sea salt and freshly ground black pepper

6 cups chicken broth

½ cup Greek-style yogurt

2 tablespoons chopped parsley and/or chives, for garnish

MAKES 6 SERVINGS

1. Melt butter in a large soup pot over medium heat. Add carrots, leek, ginger, cardamom, cinnamon, and salt and pepper to taste. Cook, stirring often until leeks are translucent, about 6 minutes; do not brown vegetables. Add broth, bring to a simmer, cover and simmer until the carrots are very tender, about 25 minutes.

2. Carefully strain vegetables from stock, reserving both. Puree the vegetables in a food processor or blender, or with an immersion blender, with enough stock to bring soup to desired consistency.

3. Return to soup pot and reheat to a bare simmer. In a small bowl, whisk yogurt vigorously with 1 tablespoon water and salt and pepper to taste. Ladle soup into serving bowls, garnish with a dollop of the yogurt and chopped herbs.

QUICK CORN AND CRAB CHOWDER

Corn and crab are natural soup mates, and with the addition of spicy Old Bay seasoning, this soup is a winner. Creamy, yet light, it makes an easy weeknight dinner teamed with a salad and a loaf of fresh bread.

2 tablespoons unsalted butter

4 scallions, trimmed and thinly sliced

1 large celery rib, diced

1 teaspoon Old Bay seasoning

1 cup chicken broth

1 cup whole milk

1 can (16 to 17 oz) whole-kernel corn, drained, liquid reserved

2 tablespoons all-purpose flour

2 round red, white, or gold potatoes, peeled and diced

8 ounces jumbo lump crabmeat, picked through to remove shells

Sea salt and freshly ground black pepper

Minced fresh parsley and chives, for garnish

MAKES 4 SERVINGS

1. Melt butter in medium soup pot over medium heat. Add scallions, celery and Old Bay seasoning and sauté until tender, about 5 minutes.

2. Meanwhile, mix broth, milk and the liquid from the canned corn; set aside.

3. Add flour to soup pot and cook, stirring constantly, for about 2 minutes. Gradually mix the broth and milk mixture into the flour mixture in the pot, whisking to incorporate each addition thoroughly before adding the next. Bring mixture to a simmer, stirring until smooth.

4. Add potatoes and simmer until tender, for 10 to 15 minutes. Add corn and crabmeat, and simmer until just heated through. Ladle soup into bowls; garnish with parsley and chives.

CELERY ROOT POTAGE

The gnarled grimy nobbiness of celery root (céleri-rave in French) makes it a prime candidate for the ugliest vegetable you ever loved. With its pronounced earthy celery flavor and dense texture, it is a natural base for creamy soups. While cream makes it extra luxurious, it is perfectly divine without embellishment.

2 tablespoons unsalted butter

1 large knob celery root (celeriac), peeled, trimmed and cubed

4 celery ribs with leaves, washed and chopped

1 leek, trimmed of dark green leaves and roots, halved lengthwise and washed, chopped

2 round red, white, or gold potatoes, peeled and cubed

6 cups chicken or vegetable broth

Sea salt and freshly ground black pepper

1 cup heavy cream (optional)

¼ cup finely chopped celery leaves, for garnish

MAKES 8 SERVINGS

1. Melt butter in a large soup pot over medium heat. Add celery root, celery, and leek, and sauté until the vegetable lose their raw look, about 5 minutes, stirring often. Add potatoes, broth, and salt and pepper. Simmer for 20 minutes partially covered, until vegetables are tender when pierced with a fork.

2. Carefully strain vegetables from liquid, reserving liquid. Puree vegetables in a food processor or blender or with an immersion blender. Add the reserved stock to thin to desired consistency. Soup may be prepared to this point and refrigerated overnight.

3. When ready to serve, reheat soup adding cream (if using). Check seasoning, garnish with chopped parsley and serve. May be served cold if desired, if so, thin to desired consistency.

CHICKEN SOUP WITH COCONUT AND LIME

Classic Thai ingredients star in this simple soup. The richness of the coconut is balanced by the heat of the jalapeño and the complex fermented salinity of fish sauce, while the lemongrass adds a beautiful citrus perfume.

1 boneless, skinless chicken thigh, diced in 1½-inch pieces

Sea salt

2 cups chicken broth

1 can (14 oz) coconut milk

1 stalk lemongrass, cut into 2-inch pieces and smashed

Juice of 1 lime

1 tablespoon Thai fish sauce

½ jalapeño chile, finely minced, or more to taste

½ cup drained canned straw mushrooms (available in the Asian section of the market)

Freshly ground black pepper

1 tablespoon finely chopped cilantro

½ scallion, white and green parts, roots trimmed, finely chopped

MAKES 4 SERVINGS

1. Season the diced chicken meat liberally with salt; set aside.

2. Combine chicken broth, coconut milk and lemongrass in a large saucepan. Bring to a lively simmer and cook for 10 minutes. Strain lemongrass from stock.

3. Add lime juice, fish sauce, chile, chicken meat and mushrooms to saucepan and continue to simmer for about 10 minutes, until chicken is cooked through. Check for seasoning, adding salt and pepper, as needed. Serve immediately, garnished with cilantro and scallion.

ROASTED TOMATO AND FENNEL SOUP

I like to make this dairy-free vegetarian soup when tomatoes are at their end-of-summer ripeness. Look for large, meaty plum tomatoes. Caramelizing the tomato, fennel and shallot in a hot oven amplifies their sweetness, creating layers of fantastic flavor. On a hot day, you can serve the soup cold, but you might need to up the seasoning and thin with more water.

1 fennel bulb

2 large shallots, peeled, trimmed and halved

2 tablespoons plus 1 teaspoon extra virgin olive oil

8 large plum tomatoes, trimmed and halved

1 large carrot, peeled and chopped

Sea salt and freshly ground black pepper

4 cups water

MAKES 6 SERVINGS

1. Preheat oven to 400°F.

2. Trim the tough ribs from the fennel and trim the dark leafy fronds from the ribs. Reserve the fronds, discard the ribs, and cut the remaining bulbous part of the fennel lengthwise into quarters. Cut the quarters into ½-inch thick slices, reserving several slices of the tender part of the bulb for garnish. Toss fennel and shallots with 2 tablespoons of the oil and spread onto a nonstick sheet pan. Place tomatoes cut side up in with the fennel and shallots and season liberally with salt and pepper to taste. Roast for about 30 minutes, until vegetables start to sizzle and caramelize on their edges. Remove pan from oven.

3. While vegetables are cooking in the oven, heat remaining oil in a soup pot over medium heat. Sauté carrots, sprinkled with about 2 tablespoons of the reserved fennel fronds, stirring often until softened, about 5 minutes.

4. Scrape the roasted vegetables into the soup pot, including all of the accumulated juices. Add water, salt and pepper to taste to the pot. Simmer over medium heat to blend flavors, about 10 minutes, stirring often. Adjust seasoning.

5. Puree the soup in a blender in batches, or in the pot with an immersion blender. Reheat and serve immediately garnished with some very finely chopped fennel fronds and bulb or allow to cool, refrigerating and serving the next day reheated or cold.

CARAMELIZED ONION SOUP

Slowly simmered, thyme-flecked, caramelized onions melt lazily into soup—nothing could be simpler nor more delicious. My rendition of a classic French onion soup will warm your soul and fill your house with fantastic aromas. Make it the day before if you can, as the flavor improves over time.

3 tablespoons unsalted butter

4 large Spanish onions, peeled, quartered, and thinly sliced

Sea salt and freshly ground black pepper

1 tablespoon chopped fresh thyme leaves

2 tablespoons all-purpose flour

½ cup dry white wine

6 cups chicken or vegetable broth

4 slices French bread, toasted

1 garlic clove, peeled and halved lengthwise

¼ cup freshly grated Parmigiano cheese

Chopped flat-leaf parsley, for garnish

MAKES 4 SERVINGS

1. Melt butter in a large saucepan or small soup pot over medium heat until sizzling but not browned. Add onions, salt, pepper and thyme and stir to coat onions with butter. Reduce heat to medium-low, cover and cook onions until very soft and caramelized, 30 to 45 minutes, stirring often.

2. Remove lid, sprinkle onions with flour, stirring well for 3 minutes to cook the flour. Add wine and broth and simmer, partially covered and stirring often, until the soup is delicately thickened and clear, about 20 minutes. Adjust seasoning.

3. Preheat a broiler. Rub toasted bread slices with cut side of garlic clove. Put on broiler tray. Sprinkle each slice of bread with a tablespoon of cheese and broil until bubbly. Place a slice of bread in serving bowl and ladle soup over bread. Garnish with parsley.

WARM GOAT CHEESE SALAD WITH MUSTARD VINAIGRETTE

Warm walnut-crusted goat cheese served on a chilled bed of greens dressed with a spicy Dijon vinaigrette will immediately transport you to a small bistrot in Paris. Open a bottle of Beaujolais, light a candle and play Carla Bruni on the stereo. Très français!

½ cup walnut pieces

½ cup unseasoned fresh breadcrumbs

1½ small logs (5 or 6 oz each) fresh chèvre (mild goat cheese), well chilled

1 egg, beaten in a small bowl

6 small handfuls of baby salad greens

1 bunch fresh chives, chopped

2 tablespoons Mustard Vinaigrette (page 75)

MAKES 6 SERVINGS

1. Process walnuts and breadcrumbs in pulses in a food processor equipped with a steel blade to fine crumbs; transfer to a plate.

2. Slice cheese into 6 (1-inch-thick) cylinders, using a sharp thin-bladed knife that has been warmed in hot water and thoroughly dried (this will keep the knife from sticking). Dip each disk of cheese into the beaten egg and then roll gently in the walnut-crumb mixture. Place crumbed cheese slices onto a cookie sheet lined with foil and chill for 1 hour (can be prepared up to 4 hours ahead).

3. Preheat oven to 375°F and bake cheese disks in the preheated oven, until speckled and lightly brown, 10 to 15 minutes.

4. As soon as the cheese is done baking, toss salad greens with vinaigrette and divide evenly onto 6 plates. Top each salad with a slice of warm cheese, sprinkle with chives and serve.

CUCUMBER SALAD

English seedless cucumbers are my favorite salad cucumbers, as they are lower in moisture, resulting in a crisper, less watery salad. I especially like the combination of dill and mint with the cool cucumber flavor. Make this salad the day before if time permits, to allow the flavors to marry.

4 large cucumbers, peeled, seeded and sliced

½ red onion peeled, very thinly sliced, rinsed in cold water and drained

3 tablespoons finely chopped fresh dill

3 tablespoons finely chopped fresh mint leaves

1 teaspoon sea salt

¼ cup white wine vinegar

2 teaspoons sugar

1½ tablespoons vegetable oil

MAKES 6 SERVINGS

Combine all ingredients in a large bowl. Mix well and refrigerate for at least 30 minutes or as long as 24 hours. (4 to 6 hours is best.) Adjust the seasoning and serve well chilled.

RINSING RAW ONION

I adore the flavor of raw onion but don't want it to overpower other flavors. Rinsing them in cold water tames their harshest flavors just enough to make them palatable when you are serving onions raw. Place the sliced or chopped onion in a small strainer and rinse it well under cold running water, or place it in a bowl of cold water, swirl it around and then drain and rinse it in a small strainer.

POTATO SALAD VINAIGRETTE

I love potato salad but not mayonnaise, so this is my version of the perfect summer potato salad. It is best served at room temperature the day it is made but can be made ahead of time and brought back to room temperature prior to serving. I like to make this salad early in the day and allow it to sit on the counter until I serve it, to give the potatoes time to soak up the piquant vinaigrette.

8   medium all-purpose potatoes
    (such as red bliss)

    Sea salt and freshly
    ground pepper

1   bunch scallions, trimmed of
    roots, finely chopped including
    tender greens

2   tablespoons coarse-grain
    Dijon mustard

3   tablespoons white wine vinegar

¼   cup extra virgin olive oil

MAKES 6 SERVINGS

1. Boil the potatoes in salted water until fork tender, about 20 minutes. Do not overcook. Drain potatoes well and cool for 30 minutes. Cut the cooled potatoes into eighths, leaving the skins on. Toss with the scallions in a medium to large serving bowl.

2. To make the vinaigrette, whisk the mustard, salt and pepper in a small mixing bowl. Whisk in vinegar until well combined and add the oil slowly while whisking constantly until the dressing is smooth and lightly thickened. Toss with the potatoes and scallion. Taste for seasoning, adding more salt and pepper to taste. Serve at room temperature.

BLACK BEAN SALAD

1   can (19 oz) black beans, drained and rinsed

1   red or yellow bell pepper, stemmed, seeded, and chopped in ¼-inch pieces

1   teaspoon minced seeded jalapeño chile

½   red onion, finely chopped, rinsed in cold water and drained

2   plum tomatoes, cored and chopped in ¼-inch pieces

½   large jicama, peeled and chopped in ¼-inch pieces

1   garlic clove, minced or finely grated on a Microplane (see page 33)

½   teaspoon ground cumin

½   teaspoon chili powder

Juice of 2 limes

1   tablespoon sherry vinegar

2   tablespoons extra virgin olive oil

Sea salt and freshly ground black pepper

2   tablespoons finely chopped fresh cilantro or parsley

I love bean salads in every cuisine. In Italy, they are prepared with white beans, in the southern USA with limas, and here, a Latino version features black beans. Bean salads can be made a day to several days in advance and refrigerated; the flavors just get better. Make sure to let them lose their chill at room temp for a little while before serving, otherwise the beans tend to get woody and the oil congealed. They are ideal as a buffet/BBQ/party dish.

MAKES 4 SERVINGS

Combine all ingredients in large bowl and mix well to blend. Set aside for at least an hour to allow flavors to mingle. This salad may be prepared several hours or up to 24 hours in advance; if so, refrigerate and remove from the refrigerator about an hour before serving.

ARUGULA SALAD WITH SHAVED PARMIGIANO AND LEMON

When a recipe is this simple, every ingredient is important. The arugula must be firm and fresh, the sea salt flaky and bright, and the cheese has to be the real stuff. Only a well-aged wedge of nutty Parmigiano-Reggiano will do. Take care with your ingredients and this salad practically prepares itself.

Juice of ½ lemon

Sea salt and freshly ground black pepper

1 tablespoon plus 2 teaspoons extra virgin olive oil

2 bunches of arugula, roots trimmed, leaves cleaned and dried

2 ounces Parmigiano-Reggiano cheese, shaved (use a "Y" shaped vegetable peeler)

Balsamic Glaze, for garnish (available at specialty food stores), or make your own.

MAKES 4 SERVINGS

1. Mix the lemon juice and salt and pepper in the bottom of a salad bowl. Mix in the oil with a fork or a whisk.

2. Immediately before serving add the arugula to the bowl, toss gently until the greens are lightly glazed with dressing. Add the strips of cheese and toss gently again. Season with additional salt and freshly ground pepper, if desired. Serve immediately garnishing the plate decoratively with the balsamic glaze.

BALSAMIC GLAZE
(REDUCED BALSAMIC VINEGAR)

Simmer 2 cups balsamic vinegar in a small saucepan over low heat until the vinegar is reduced to a thick glaze, about 1 hour. Check often after the first half hour since it is more apt to scorch near the end of cooking. Makes about ¼ cup.

ELLA'S CHOPPED SALAD

My daughter, Ella, loved to brown-bag this salad for her school lunch. So naturally I loved making it for her. I was sure to always have the ingredients on hand (effortless since all of the ingredients are either canned or refrigerated staples), and throwing it together was easy. After being in the container in her lunch bag for a few hours, the flavors only improved. If I had leftover chicken or steak, that would often land in the salad as well.

1 romaine lettuce heart, core removed, cut in ½-inch pieces

2 large celery ribs, leaves trimmed, cut in ½-inch pieces

2 ripe avocados, peeled, pitted, cut in ½-inch pieces

1 can (14 oz) hearts of palm, drained, cut in ½-inch pieces

2 ripe tomatoes, cored, cut in ½-inch pieces

1 cup canned chick peas (garbanzo beans), drained

1 teaspoon fine sea salt, plus more to taste

¼ teaspoon freshly ground black pepper

Juice of 1 lemon

2 tablespoons extra virgin olive oil

¼ cup finely chopped fresh cilantro (optional)

MAKES 4 SERVINGS

1. Toss the romaine, celery, avocado, hearts of palm, tomatoes, and chick peas in a large mixing bowl. Season with salt and pepper and toss again.

2. Add the lemon juice and oil and mix gently to combine. Taste salad and adjust seasoning; mix in the cilantro (if using) and serve.

✳ NOTE: This salad can be made several hours ahead of time, holding back the romaine lettuce, covered and refrigerated. When ready to serve, add the romaine and toss well to combine.

PANTESCA SALAD

Pantelleria is a tiny island that lies at the edge of the Tyrrhenian Sea, just south of Sicily, barely 80 miles off the coast of Tunisia. It is mountainous and lush with grape vines, olives, and most famously, capers, the star of the island that grows in abundance everywhere. Pantesca salad is featured on most menus on the island, where it is eaten either as an antipasto (before the meal) or as a side salad with the meal. It is worth the effort to seek out large salt-preserved capers, which have a deeper and fuller flavor than the tiny capers that are more commonly available packed in brine.

4 round potatoes, red skinned, yellow, or white

2 tablespoons sea salt, plus more to taste

2 tablespoons salt-packed capers

¼ cup halved and pitted Italian black olives

1 teaspoon fresh oregano leaves, finely chopped

1 pint ripe cherry tomatoes, halved

¼ red onion, thinly sliced and rinsed in cold water for 1 minute

Freshly ground black pepper

1 tablespoon white wine vinegar

¼ cup extra virgin olive oil

MAKES 6 SERVINGS

1. Put the potatoes in a medium saucepan, add enough water to cover and the salt; bring to a boil over medium-high heat. Reduce heat to a simmer and cook until potatoes are just fork tender, about 20 minutes. Drain and set aside to cool.

2. While potatoes are cooking, soak the capers in cold water to wash away their salt, about 5 minutes, drain, rinse and repeat 2 times.

3. Peel the cooled potatoes and cut in quarters. Combine all ingredients, in a large mixing bowl. Toss and adjust seasoning. Serve immediately; may be made an hour or so before serving and held at room temperature.

INSALATA CAPRESE

Freshly formed mozzarella, milky and tangy, from the Sorrentine peninsula, stars in this classic summer salad from the nearby island of Capri. All you need is an abundance of ripe, sweet tomatoes, excellent-quality sea salt, and a fruity extra virgin olive oil, and you can't go wrong. If you are feeling adventurous, add a few grinds of pepper and fresh basil leaves strewn about—buono!

1 large ball (1 pound) fresh mozzarella, the best quality you can find

2 vine-ripened tomatoes, room temperature

Sea salt to taste, preferably fleur de sel

2 tablespoons extra virgin olive oil

Several basil leaves or a sprig, for garnish

MAKES 2 TO 4 SERVINGS

Slice the cheese and tomatoes. Shingle on a serving platter, alternating slices of cheese and tomato. Season liberally with salt, drizzle with oil, and garnish with basil.

SIMPLE SALAD DRESSINGS

BASIC VINAIGRETTE

MAKES ABOUT 1/2 CUP

½ garlic clove, finely chopped

½ teaspoon fine sea salt

3 tablespoons red wine vinegar

¼ cup extra virgin olive oil

1 tablespoon freshly chopped herbs, such as parsley, chives, mint, etc.

Freshly ground black pepper to taste

In a small bowl, mash garlic and salt with a fork until well combined. Mix in vinegar and whisk in olive oil. Mix in herbs and pepper, and adjust seasoning.

SHERRY ORANGE VINAIGRETTE

MAKES ABOUT 1/2 CUP

½ garlic clove, minced to a paste

½ teaspoon sea salt

Freshly ground black pepper

Juice of ½ orange

2 tablespoons sherry vinegar

¼ cup extra virgin olive oil

2 tablespoons freshly chopped herbs, a combination of parsley, chive, and mint

In a small bowl, mash garlic and salt together with a fork until well combined. Mix in orange juice and vinegar and whisk in olive oil. Mix in herbs and adjust seasoning.

MUSTARD VINAIGRETTE

MAKES ABOUT 1/2 CUP

½ garlic clove, minced

½ teaspoon fine sea salt

1 teaspoon smooth French Dijon mustard

3 tablespoons white wine vinegar

¼ cup extra virgin olive oil

1 tablespoon freshly chopped herbs, such as parsley, chives, mint, etc.

Freshly ground black pepper to taste

In a small bowl, mash garlic and salt with a fork until well combined. Mix in mustard and vinegar and whisk in olive oil. Mix in herbs and pepper, and adjust seasoning.

GREEN BEAN, TOMATO AND ORANGE SALAD

All salads are beautiful, but composed salads, with their carefully designed layers of color and texture are about beauty. This composition is particularly stunning for its unique juxtaposition of color, flavor and texture: crisp purple onions, tangy juicy crimson tomatoes, plump meaty vibrant green beans, and sweet fruity Day-Glo orange oranges. The sherry vinaigrette gives the whole a slightly Spanish flavor palate and a glistening sheen.

2 oranges, peeled and sliced away from membrane into sections

½ red onion, peeled, thinly sliced and rinsed in cold water for 1 minute

    Sea salt and freshly ground black pepper

¼ cup Sherry Orange Vinaigrette (page 75)

2 ripe tomatoes, cored and cut in thin wedges

1 pound green beans, stemmed, cooked until crisp/tender in salted water, drained and cooled

1 tablespoon of drained capers packed in brine

1 tablespoon finely chopped fresh chives

MAKES 6 SERVINGS

1. In a small mixing bowl, combine the orange segments, onion, salt and pepper to taste with 1 tablespoon of the vinaigrette, mixing well.

2. In another small mixing bowl, toss the tomato together with salt and pepper to taste and 1 tablespoon of the vinaigrette, mixing gently and thoroughly.

3. In a medium mixing bowl, mix the green beans with salt and pepper to taste and 1 tablespoon of the vinaigrette, mixing well.

4. Mound a handful of green beans onto each plate, top decoratively with orange and onion, and then with tomato wedges and chives. Season with a more salt and pepper and spoon additional vinaigrette over and around the salads.

SEARED ROMAINE HEARTS WITH LEMON AND PARMIGIANO CHEESE

Craving a salad in midwinter, I dreamed up this warm version of Caesar. I know it is missing the anchovies and garlic, but it's strong on the lemon and Parmigiano components. Pan searing the romaine gives it a sweet, nutty flavor that I adore. In warmer months, I prepare this outside on the side burners of my gas grill.

2 tablespoons extra virgin olive oil

1 large head of romaine lettuce, washed, dried and trimmed slightly, sliced lengthwise through the core, leaving core intact

Sea salt and freshly ground black pepper

Juice of ½ lemon

⅛ cup freshly grated Parmigiano-Reggiano cheese (use a Microplane; see page 33)

MAKES 2 SERVINGS

1. Heat the oil in a large, heavy cast-iron frying pan over medium heat until hot, but not smoking. Season the Romaine with salt and pepper and place it cut side down in the hot pan. Allow lettuce to cook until it browns well on the cut side; it will take several minutes.

2. Flip the romaine halves onto their rounded side to brown. The leaves should become tender, and the edges will wilt. You may need to flip them a few times to keep them cooking evenly. They are done when the core can be pierced easily with the tip of a sharp knife.

3. Put on a serving platter, cut side up, drizzle with lemon juice and sprinkle with cheese, which should start to melt on contact. Serve immediately.

PASTA + RICE

SPAGHETTI WITH PIQUANT BROCCOLI

Tomato pasta sauce is so commonplace that we no longer think about what it is—pureed vegetable. Once you get that simple concept, an eggplant sauce, or this broccoli sauce, stops seeming strange. This wonderfully creamy, yet piquant combination of pecorino cheese and broccoli has a silky texture and big powerful flavors. If you are tempted to omit the anchovy I encourage you to reserve judgment until you taste. It lends an important depth of flavor that is delicious.

3 to 5 tablespoons sea salt, plus more to taste

2 pounds broccoli florets (approximately 2 bunches), large stems trimmed

½ cup extra virgin olive oil

1 small onion, finely chopped

2 to 3 garlic cloves, coarsely chopped

Pinch of crushed red pepper flakes

1 or 2 canned anchovy fillets in oil, minced

Liberal amounts of freshly ground black pepper

1 pound spaghetti

½ cup grated pecorino Romano cheese, plus additional to pass at table

MAKES 2 TO 3 ENTREE SERVINGS, 4 FIRST-COURSE SERVINGS

1. Bring two pots of water to a boil—one a large pot for pasta and the other a large saucepan or small pot for cooking the broccoli. Season both with salt.

2. When the broccoli water boils, add the broccoli and cook until very tender, about 10 minutes. Drain, but reserve 2 cups of the broccoli cooking water.

3. Meanwhile, heat the olive oil in a large saucepan or deep sauté pan over medium heat. Add onion and sauté until it loses its raw look, about 1 minute. Add garlic, pepper flakes and anchovy, sautéing until the anchovy starts to dissolve, about 2 minutes more.

4. Add the broccoli and the reserved broccoli cooking liquid. Cook, crushing the broccoli with a wooden spoon as it cooks. Add the black pepper. Increase heat to medium-high and simmer sauce for 8 to 10 minutes, until lightly thickened. Add additional water if needed to keep the sauce flowing.

5. While the sauce is simmering, boil the pasta according to package directions. Drain the pasta and reserve ¾ cup of pasta cooking water.

6. Add the drained pasta to the sauce and toss to coat. Add some reserved pasta water as needed to keep the sauce flowing. Adjust seasoning and garnish with cheese; serve immediately, passing extra cheese at table.

PERCIATELLI WITH TOMATO, PANCETTA AND ONION

Perciatelli is fat holy spaghetti; holy both physically (it's got a hole in it) and spiritually (it originated in the capital of the Holy Roman Empire). The channel that runs through the middle of each pasta tube encloses a thin trail of my all time favorite spicy sauce. Named "Amatriciana," it is traditionally prepared with guanciale, an unsmoked bacon made from pig jowl or cheek that is difficult to find in the US. Pancetta (unsmoked pork belly) is a fine substitute.

3 tablespoons sea salt,
  plus more to taste

¼ cup extra virgin olive oil

1 tablespoon unsalted butter
  (optional)

  Pinch of crushed red
  pepper flakes

2 (¼-inch-thick) slices pancetta,
  cut in ½-inch pieces

1 onion, diced

2 garlic cloves, finely chopped

1 can (28 oz) whole tomatoes,
  preferably San Marzano, drained

  Freshly ground black pepper

1 pound perciatelli or spaghetti

½ cup freshly grated Parmigiano-
  Reggiano cheese

1 tablespoon flat-leaf parsley,
  chopped fine

MAKES 2 TO 3 ENTREE SERVINGS, 4 FIRST-COURSE SERVINGS

1. Bring a large pot of water for pasta to a boil. Season with salt.

2. Meanwhile, heat the olive oil and butter (if using), in a large saucepan or deep sauté pan over medium-low heat. Add pepper flakes (to taste) and pancetta and sauté, stirring often until pancetta is cooked but not brown.

3. Add onion and sauté until translucent, about 5 minutes. Add garlic, sautéing until aromatic, about 2 minutes more. Add tomatoes, crushing with your hands as you add them to the pot. Add salt and black pepper to taste. Increase heat to medium-high and boil sauce until lightly thickened, 8 to 10 minutes, stirring often.

4. While the sauce is simmering, boil the pasta according to package directions. Drain the pasta and reserve ¾ cup of pasta cooking water.

5. Add the drained pasta to the sauce and toss to coat. Add some reserved pasta water as needed to keep the sauce flowing. Adjust seasoning and garnish with cheese and chopped parsley; serve immediately.

TAGLIATELLE CON RAGÙ

Pasta with meat sauce is my go-to soul food. If I had to choose a last meal, this would be it! In Italy, a ragu simply means a sauce prepared with meat, often with vegetables. Tagliatelle is a long flat ribbon of pasta, similar to but narrower than fettuccine. Ask your butcher to grind the meats fresh for you and take care to season the sauce every step of the way—you will be deliciously rewarded. Open a bottle of Chianti, take a bite, close your eyes, and enjoy the Tuscan landscape!

1 tablespoon extra virgin olive oil

1 tablespoon unsalted butter

1 small onion, finely chopped

½ teaspoon crushed red pepper flakes, or to taste

2 garlic cloves, finely chopped

1 celery rib, finely chopped

1 carrot, finely chopped

Sea salt and ground black pepper

1 pound "meatloaf/meatball blend" (⅔ ground beef, ⅓ ground pork, ⅓ ground veal), or any single meat

1 cup dry red wine

2 cups canned plum tomatoes, preferably San Marzano, drained

¼ cup chopped flat-leaf parsley

1 pound tagliatelle

Freshly grated Parmigiano-Reggiano cheese

MAKES 2 TO 3 ENTREE SERVINGS, 4 FIRST-COURSE SERVINGS

1. Heat oil and butter in a heavy, deep pot overmedium heat. Sauté onion, pepper flakes, garlic, celery, and carrot until barely tender, about 5 minutes. Do not brown. Season with salt and pepper to taste.

2. Add the meat, season with more salt and pepper, and sauté until meat loses its raw red color, about 5 minutes. Add the wine and cook until wine evaporates.

3. Add the tomatoes, crushing them with your hands, season with more salt and pepper, and simmer gently until thickened, about 30 minutes, stirring often.

4. While sauce is simmering, boil a large pot full of water for pasta. Add 3 tablespoons salt to pasta water. Boil pasta according to package directions, draining the pasta a minute or so early, when it is still slightly underdone.

5. Reserve 2 cups pasta cooking water. Drain pasta and add to pot of sauce gradually, tossing as you add more pasta, until all of pasta has been added to sauce. Add cheese to taste and just enough pasta cooking water to make a flowing sauce. Pass additional cheese with pasta at the table.

PENNE PASTA PUTTANESCA

Rumor has it that in Rome, ladies of the evening *(puttane),* who were voraciously hungry after a long night on the job would come home and prepare pasta using staples that they had on hand in the pantry, such as anchovies, garlic, capers, olives, and tinned tomatoes. The resulting pasta dish, which is lusty and full of bold flavors, was named for those hard-working gals.

1 pound good-quality dried penne

Extra virgin olive oil to coat bottom of pan

1 small onion, finely chopped

2 to 3 garlic cloves, coarsely chopped

Crushed red pepper flakes

2 oil-packed anchovy filets

1 can (28 oz) whole tomatoes, preferably San Marzano, drained

2 tablespoons small whole capers in brine (drained)

¼ cup pitted and chopped good-quality Italian black olives

Liberal amounts of freshly ground black pepper

3 tablespoons sea salt, plus more to taste

2 tablespoons chopped flat-leaf parsley, plus more for garnish

1½ cup grated pecorino Romano cheese

MAKES 2 TO 3 ENTREE SERVINGS, 4 FIRST-COURSE SERVINGS

1. Bring a large pot of water for pasta to a boil. Meanwhile, heat olive oil in a large saucepan or deep sauté pan over medium heat. Add onion and sauté just until it loses its raw look, about a minute, stirring as needed. Add garlic, pepper flakes (to taste) and anchovy and continue to sauté for several minutes until anchovy starts to dissolve. Do not allow vegetables to brown; the onion should be translucent.

2. Add tomatoes, crushing with your hands as they are added to the pot. Add capers, olives and black pepper. Increase heat to medium-high and boil sauce until lightly thickened, 8 to 10 minutes, stirring often.

3. While the sauce is simmering, add the salt to the pasta water and boil the pasta according to package directions. Drain the pasta a minute or so early, when it is still slightly underdone. Reserve ¾ cup of pasta cooking water.

4. Add the drained pasta to the sauce, and toss to coat. Add some reserved pasta water as needed to keep the sauce flowing. Adjust seasoning and garnish with cheese and chopped parsley; serve immediately.

SPAGHETTI WITH SPINACH AND FETA

I made up this Greek-inspired pasta dish for my daughter, Ella, one night, when she asked for "pasta, cheesy and garlicky," using ingredients I had on hand: a fresh tomato, some garlic, half a bag of baby spinach, and some Greek feta cheese. A family favorite was born.

3   tablespoons sea salt

¼   cup extra virgin olive oil

    Pinch of crushed red pepper flakes

2   garlic cloves, finely chopped

1   vine ripened tomato, chopped

½   cup water

8   ounces baby spinach, chopped

1   pound spaghetti

1   cup crumbled Greek feta cheese

    Freshly ground black pepper

MAKES 2 TO 3 ENTREE SERVINGS, 4 FIRST-COURSE SERVINGS

1. Bring a large pot of water for pasta to a boil. Season with salt.

2. Meanwhile, heat the olive oil in a large saucepan or deep sauté pan over medium heat. Add pepper flakes (to taste) and garlic and sauté, stirring often until the garlic is fragrant, about 1 minute. Do not allow the garlic to brown!

3. Add tomato and water, and cook until the tomato starts to soften into a sauce, about 5 minutes. Stir in the spinach and cook just long enough to wilt the leaves, about 2 minutes. Set sauce aside while preparing pasta.

4. Boil the pasta according to package directions, draining the pasta a minute or so early, when it is still slightly underdone, and reserving 2 cups of pasta cooking water.

5. Return saucepan with sauce to medium heat. Add the drained pasta to the sauce in three or four additions, alternating with feta cheese, continually stirring to coat the pasta evenly with sauce. Add the reserved pasta water as needed to keep the sauce flowing. Pour into a serving bowl, grind pepper over top, and serve immediately.

GREEK-STYLE ORZO SALAD

Typically, I don't love pasta salads. They tend to be bland and pasty, but this delicious salad bursts with the sunshine of a Greek island. Loaded with raw spinach, feta cheese, olives and sun-dried tomatoes, this is a filling and healthy salad for a light lunch or served as an accompaniment to grilled and roasted meats, chicken and fish. Good news alert: the flavors only improve over time, which makes this the perfect picnic or buffet salad!

2   tablespoons sea salt

½   pound orzo pasta

1   cup pitted kalamata olives, chopped

¼   cup sun-dried tomatoes packed in oil, drained and finely chopped

1   cup crumbled Greek feta cheese

1   bunch spinach, washed, dried, thick stems trimmed, leaves thinly sliced

2   tablespoons chopped fresh dill

1   garlic clove, minced

    Juice and finely grated zest of 1 lemon

¼   cup white wine vinegar

¼   cup extra virgin olive oil

    Sea salt and freshly ground black pepper

MAKES 6 SERVINGS

1. Bring a large pot of water for to a boil. Season with salt, add orzo and cook according to package directions. Drain and rinse with cold water. Transfer to a large mixing bowl.

2. Add the remaining ingredients and toss to combine. Taste for seasoning and refrigerate for at least 4 hours. Remove from the refrigerator at least an hour before serving.

PEELING GARLIC

One of the simplest methods on earth for peeling garlic is to simply lay the unpeeled clove on a cutting board, take a chefs knife with the blade on its side and lay the knife over the garlic clove. Give the side of the knife a good whack—the garlic clove will be slightly smashed and the peel will slip off effortlessly. This method works perfectly whether you intend to chop, mince, grate, or leave the garlic cloves whole.

SOBA NOODLE SALAD WITH SESAME, SOY AND GINGER

Asian flavors are perfect for this quick and savory noodle salad. I love planning on this dish for a buffet. It can be prepared the day before and actually improves with age! If you don't have traditional soba noodles, feel free to substitute spaghetti.

3   tablespoons sea salt, plus more to taste

1   package (8 oz) soba noodles

1   garlic clove, minced

1   tablespoon peeled and finely grated gingerroot

¼   cup soy sauce

1   tablespoon rice vinegar

    Juice of 1 lime

1   teaspoon sugar

¼   teaspoon chili paste (optional)

¼   cup blended oil or vegetable oil

1   teaspoon toasted sesame oil

2   scallions, roots trimmed and thinly sliced

2   tablespoons toasted sesame seeds (see note)

MAKES 4 SERVINGS

1. Bring a large pot of water for pasta to a boil. Season with salt, add soba and cook according to package directions. Drain and rinse with cold water. Transfer to a large mixing bowl.

2. In a separate bowl mix the garlic, ginger, soy sauce, vinegar, lime juice, sugar, and chili paste (if using). Whisk in the oils and pour over the noodles.

3. Add the scallions and sesame seeds and toss to combine. Taste for seasoning, and add more salt if necessary. May be prepared the day before and refrigerated.

* NOTE: To toast sesame seeds or nuts, simply warm a small nonstick skillet over medium heat and cook seeds or nuts, stirring and swirling constantly, until the seeds or nuts are golden brown. Keep an eye on them and remove from heat as soon as they start to color—the process seems to happen very quickly and they burn in the blink of an eye!

HERBED COUSCOUS

Originally a Berber pasta dish, couscous is often sold as grain but is actually tiny bits of semolina pasta. It is simple to prepare and takes on the flavor of whatever it is cooked with. This fresh, light side dish is inundated with herbs and sparked with a hit of lemon juice. Serve with roasted chicken, white meats, or grilled seafood.

1 tablespoon extra virgin olive oil

1 scallion, roots trimmed, finely chopped

1 cup quick-cooking couscous

Sea salt and freshly ground black pepper

1 cup boiling water

1 tablespoon chopped fresh herbs, mint, parsley and/or chives

Juice of ½ lemon

MAKES 4 SERVINGS

1. Heat olive oil in a medium saucepan over medium heat. Add scallion and sauté until wilted, being careful not to burn, about 1 minute. Add couscous and stir to coat with the oil. Season with salt and pepper.

2. Add boiling water, herbs, and lemon juice, stir well, cover, and remove from heat. Wait 8 minutes and fluff with a fork; serve immediately.

MOROCCAN SPICED COUSCOUS SALAD

4 cups vegetable or chicken broth

2 cups quick-cooking couscous

½ cup currants

1 can (14 oz) chick peas (garbanzo beans), drained and rinsed

1 can (14 oz) pitted black olives, drained and finely chopped

2 carrots, peeled and finely chopped

1 cup frozen peas, thawed

1 cup whole almonds, toasted and chopped

2 scallions, trimmed of roots, finely chopped

1 garlic clove, minced or pressed

½ teaspoon finely grated gingerroot

¼ teaspoon ground cumin

¼ teaspoon ground coriander

¼ teaspoon ground cinnamon

¼ teaspoon ground turmeric

2 teaspoons sea salt

½ teaspoon ground cayenne pepper, or more or less to taste

½ cup chopped flat-leaf parsley

½ cup chopped cilantro leaves

Finely grated zest of 1 lemon and the juice of 2 lemons

3 tablespoons extra virgin olive oil

Sea salt and freshly ground black pepper

Couscous, the teeny tiny pasta from Morocco, is precooked so all you have to do to "cook" it is soak it in hot liquid—easy. It is a wonderful vehicle for the spicy, slightly exotic flavors in this perfect party dish. Like all pasta salads, it gets better when made ahead of time and is a fabulous bed for grilled meats, shellfish or fish.

MAKES 8 SERVINGS

1. Bring the broth to a boil. Put the couscous in a large mixing bowl and add the hot broth. Stir to moisten the couscous, cover and set aside until the couscous has absorbed all of the liquid, about 8 minutes. Uncover and cool to room temperature.

2. Combine remaining ingredients with cooled couscous and toss well. Taste for seasoning and add additional salt and pepper if necessary. Serve immediately or refrigerate overnight.

COCONUT RICE

Perfectly cooked buttery white rice is like a little black dress—just the right thing when nothing else quite fits the occasion. This classic number is embellished with a soupçon of exotica. The rice is perfumed with jasmine, and coconut flavor is infused into the grain in two ways—the rice is simmered in lite coconut milk, and garnished with shredded coconut.

1 cup white jasmine rice

½ teaspoon unsalted butter

1 can (13.5 oz) lite coconut milk

½ cup water

1 teaspoon sea salt

3 tablespoons dried shredded coconut

MAKES 4 SERVINGS

1. Put the rice in a strainer and rinse under cold running water until the water runs clear, about 2 minutes. Drain well.

2. Melt the butter in a medium saucepan with a lid over medium heat. Add the rice and stir to coat all of the rice grains with butter. Sauté the rice for several minutes until it starts to smell nutty; do not allow it to color.

3. Add coconut milk, water, salt, and 2 tablespoons of the shredded coconut, stirring well. Cover pot and cook at a low simmer until rice is tender and swollen, about 18 minutes.

4. While the rice is cooking, heat a heavy frying pan (not nonstick) over high heat until very hot. Turn off the heat and add the coconut. Stir quickly until the coconut is lightly toasted, about 1 minute. Pour onto a plate.

5. When the rice is done cooking, fluff with a fork and serve garnished with the toasted coconut.

RISOTTO PARMIGIANO

I know you've heard stories. Risotto takes hours of stirring and if you don't know what you're doing you will end up with a pot of paste. Do not fear! You can make a risotto while the rest of your meal is roasting or resting. The 18 minutes pass quickly and the labor required is minimal and oh so worth it. If you are feeling particularly indulgent, drizzle a bit of truffle oil over the finished dish.

3   tablespoons unsalted butter, plus additional for finishing dish

2   tablespoons olive oil

2   tablespoons finely chopped onion

Sea salt and freshly ground black pepper

1½ cups Arborio rice

5   cups chicken broth, simmering

½   cup freshly grated Parmigiano-Reggiano cheese, plus additional for finishing dish

¼   teaspoon white truffle oil, for garnish (optional)

MAKES 4 FIRST-COURSE SERVINGS

1. Melt 1 tablespoon of the butter and the olive oil in a large heavy saucepan over medium heat. Add the onion and sauté until translucent. Season with salt and pepper, add the rice, and stir until each grain of rice is coated with butter/oil.

2. Add ½ cup of simmering broth. Stir until the broth is nearly absorbed. Add the rest of the broth, ½ cup at a time, stirring and waiting until each addition of broth is almost completely absorbed before adding the next. Total cooking time should be approximately 18 minutes. In the last few minutes of cooking, when the rice grains are resilient to the bite and swimming in silky sauce, remove from the heat, stir in the remaining butter and the cheese. Adjust seasoning with salt and pepper and serve immediately, drizzled with truffle oil, if desired. Pass additional cheese at the table.

SAFFRON RICE PILAF WITH TOASTED ALMONDS

The fragrance of saffron is subtle—a mixture of flowers and fruit, but its color is knock out. If the brilliance of sunlight could be made solid it would be saffron. Such extravagance doesn't come cheap. Saffron is the most expensive spice on earth, but if you consider that each strand is hand-harvested from the interior of a crocus blossom, and that there are literally thousands of strands in every ounce, the cost seems justified. Saffron and rice are long-time companions, and rightly so, for no other ingredient shows off this seasoning better than perfectly simmered long-grain rice.

4 cups chicken broth

¼ teaspoon saffron threads

2 cups long-grain white rice, such as basmati

1 tablespoon extra virgin olive oil

1 small onion, finely chopped

Sea salt and freshly ground black pepper

1 tablespoons toasted almonds, coarsely chopped

1 tablespoon finely chopped flat-leaf parsley

MAKES 4 SERVINGS

1. Heat the chicken broth and the saffron in a small pot over medium-low heat until it simmers. Turn off the heat.

2. Meanwhile, put the rice in a strainer and rinse under cold running water until the water runs clear, about 2 minutes. Drain well.

3. Heat the oil in a medium saucepan over medium heat. Add the onion and sauté until translucent, about 3 minutes. Season with salt and pepper to taste. Add the rinsed rice and stir until the grains of rice are lightly toasted, about 3 minutes.

4. Add the saffron-infused chicken broth, stir the rice well, cover, and cook at a low simmer until the rice is tender, about 18 minutes.

5. Remove from the heat and set aside for 5 minutes. Fluff with a fork and serve garnished with the almonds and parsley.

MEAT + POULTRY

NANA'S HAMBURGERS

I know burgers aren't Jewish food, but my nana didn't. For 98 years (I assume she started cooking at birth) Nana made the best Russian/Jewish-style burgers in the world. She started by going to the butcher, selected a chuck roast and had it ground to order. She blended it with onion, matzo meal and egg—somewhere in between burger and meatloaf. We ate them topped with fried onions and sautéed canned mushrooms, without a bun.

1   small all-purpose potato, peeled and coarsely chopped

1   small yellow onion, coarsely chopped

1   large or extra large egg

1   pound ground beef chuck

3   tablespoons matzo meal or unflavored breadcrumbs

    Sea salt and freshly ground black pepper

2   tablespoons vegetable oil

MAKES 6 SERVINGS

1. Blend potato, onion and egg in a blender or food processor until liquefied.

2. In a large mixing bowl, mix the beef, potato mixture, 2 tablespoons of the matzo meal, and salt and pepper to taste. Form mixture into 4 oval patties and sprinkle the top with the remaining matzo meal. Form a crosshatch pattern on top of the burgers, using a butter knife, not cutting into the burgers, just forming a slight impression.

3. Heat oil in a large sauté pan over medium heat. Season the burgers with salt and pepper and sauté the burgers until golden brown and cooked through, about 7 minutes per side. Serve immediately or cool, refrigerate and reheat gently.

STRIP STEAKS GRILLED WITH MY DAD'S STEAK SAUCE

My father gave me this recipe. I'm sure he clipped it from a long-gone, nameless newspaper, and even though I know he didn't create it, in my mind it will always be his special steak sauce. I make it in bulk and keep it in a huge jar in my fridge (as does he), using it to marinate whatever I have on hand—chicken, beef or pork. My steaks consider it a privilege to bathe in this sauce overnight. It is clearly the best steak sauce I've ever had! Thanks Dad.

4 sirloin strip steaks (about 8 ounces each), at least 1 inch thick, excess fat trimmed

2 cups Dad's Steak Sauce

DAD'S STEAK SAUCE

MAKES A LOT (ABOUT 8 CUPS)

1 bottle (15 oz) soy sauce

1 bottle (10 oz) A-1 steak sauce

1 bottle (10 oz) Lea and Perrin's Worcestershire sauce

1 bottle (14 oz) Heinz ketchup

2 tablespoons Dijon mustard

2 tablespoons Crystal hot pepper sauce

Juice of 2 lemons

1 cup dark brown sugar

1 tablespoon garlic powder

1 tablespoon celery salt

MAKES 4 LARGE SERVINGS

1. Put the steaks and sauce in a zipper-lock bag; squeeze out excess air, seal and refrigerate for at least 4 hours or overnight.

2. Preheat a grill to medium-high. Remove steaks from the bag, drain excess sauce from steaks, and pat dry with a paper towel.

3. Brush grill grate with a wire brush and rub the clean grate liberally with oil. Grill the steaks until browned on the surface and slightly charred at the edges. An instant-read thermometer inserted into the side of the thickest steak should read 130°F for medium-rare results. This will take 5 to 8 minutes per side. Allow steaks to rest for 10 minutes, loosely covered, before serving.

NORMA'S LONDON BROIL WITH RED WINE MARINADE

This London broil recipe is my mother's. I grew up with a flat Tupperware container in the refrigerator that held a London broil, soaking in a tangy red wine marinade. Every day my mother would flip the container, infusing the meat with flavor while it tenderized. The flavors imparted by the marinade are fabulous. Leftover London broil, thinly sliced against the grain, is a favorite for sandwiches in our house.

2   garlic cloves, smashed

1   teaspoon sea salt

1   tablespoon smooth Dijon mustard

2   tablespoons ketchup

1   cup red wine

2   tablespoons soy sauce

1   tablespoon Worcestershire sauce

2½ tablespoons fresh lemon juice

¼   cup extra virgin olive oil

2   tablespoons herbes de Provence or Italian seasoning

    Additional sea salt and freshly ground black pepper

1   top round London broil, weighing about 2 pounds

MAKES 4 SERVINGS WITH LEFTOVERS

1. For the marinade, mix the garlic, salt, mustard and ketchup in a mixing bowl with a fork. Add everything else except for the meat. Put the London broil in a large zipper-lock bag or container and add the marinade. Turn to coat and seal; refrigerate for at least 24 or up to 72 hours.

2. Preheat grill on high. Remove London broil from marinade. Scrub the grill grate and coat with oil. Grill meat to desired degree of doneness, about 7 minutes per side for rare. Put on a cutting board and allow to rest for 5 minutes. Cut in thin slices against the grain.

SOUTH PHILLY–STYLE MEATBALLS

3 slices good-quality fresh Italian bread (seedless)

4 garlic cloves, finely chopped

1 heaping tablespoon chopped flat-leaf parsley

½ cup milk

3 tablespoons extra virgin olive oil

1 yellow onion, finely chopped

Sea salt and ground black pepper

Crushed red pepper flakes

1 can (28 oz) San Marzano tomatoes and their juice

1 can (28 oz) San Marzano tomato puree

3 tablespoons good-quality tomato paste

2 cups water

2 large or extra large eggs

1½ lbs ground beef sirloin or "meatloaf/meatball blend" (⅔ ground beef, ⅓ ground pork, ⅓ ground veal)

½ cup freshly grated Parmigiano cheese

1 bay leaf

When I was a kid, going "downtown" for Italian meant only one thing and everyone knew it—South Philadelphia—the land of big-haired waitresses ("What'll it be, Hon?") with little patience and a big sense of humor. You could always count on two things—the bread and the meatballs. The bread was impeccably fresh, chewy-crusty, studded with sesame seeds, and most likely from the bakery next door. The meatballs were oversized, tender, garlicky, and swimming in gravy (South Philly for tomato sauce). Sundays in our house usually involved a huge pot of sauce with my mom's version of those amazing meatballs that had been simmering for hours in the pot. Part of what makes this pot of meat and sauce so delicious is that the meat is cooked entirely in the sauce, forcing all of the flavors to blend together. None of the meat jus is lost by precooking.

MAKES 6 SERVINGS

1. Put the bread in a large mixing bowl. Sprinkle with half the garlic and the parsley. Add the milk and move the bread around to moisten completely. Set aside for 10 to 15 minutes, while you prepare the sauce.

2. Heat a large pot on medium heat and add the olive oil. Add the onions, season with salt, black pepper and pepper flakes (to taste), and sauté until the onions start to look translucent. Don't brown the onions! Add the tomatoes and their juice, crushing them with your fingers as you add them to the pot. Add the tomato puree, the paste and the water, stirring well to incorporate. Season with salt and pepper to taste. Add the bay leaf and the remaining garlic and bring the mixture to a lively simmer, stirring often.

3. For the meatballs: break up the wet bread mixture with a fork until it is completely mushy. Add the eggs and mix together well. Add the meat, cheese, and salt and pepper to taste and mix until well combined. Form the meat mixture into balls. I like larger than golf ball size meatballs, but there are no rules here. If you prefer small meatballs, feel free.

4. As you roll the meatballs by hand, drop them gently into the simmering pot of sauce. I drop them in so that they are still half in and half out of the sauce, so that I can see where there is still space for another ball. I start on the outside of the pot, making a circular pattern around the exterior of the pot to insure that I can fit the maximum amount of meatballs into the pot. If you just were to drop the balls into the pot anywhere, you wouldn't remember where the spaces were. I don't require this type of order in every area of my life, but when it comes to cooking the meatballs, there is order in my court.

5. Cook the meatballs in the simmering sauce, partially covered, for about 2 hours, stirring gently, about every 15 minutes, being careful not to break up the meatballs, I have been known to toss some browned spicy Italian sausage and/or some country-style pork spare-ribs (on the bone) into the pot (totally optional). As the sauce cooks, use a ladle to skim any extra fat from the surface of the sauce. When the meatballs are firm and cooked through (and the pork is falling-apart tender, if used) and the entire house smells delicious, it is time to eat! One of the best parts of this dish is that it only improves in flavor when eaten the next day, making it ideal for larger gatherings.

CHARRED STEAK SALAD WITH MUSTARD AND GREENS

2 tablespoons Dijon mustard

¼ cup dry red wine

1 garlic clove, finely chopped
or pressed

2 tablespoons chopped flat-leaf
Italian parsley

Pinch of sea salt

Fresh ground black pepper

4 filet steaks or NY strip steaks
(4 to 6 ounces each if filet,
8 to 10 ounces each if strip)

SALAD

2 teaspoons Dijon mustard

2 teaspoons red wine vinegar

Pinch of sea salt

Freshly ground black pepper

½ cup extra virgin olive oil

¼ cup chopped fresh herbs, such
as parsley, chives, and/or mint

2 ripe tomatoes, cored and chopped

2 scallions, roots trimmed,
finely chopped

4 cups mixed salad greens

Juicy slices of charred garlicky steak sitting warm on top of cold crisp greens, herbs and ripe tomatoes dressed sparingly in spicy red wine vinaigrette could be the best part of summer. If you're pressed for time, skip marinating the steak, the salad will still shine. It also a great use for leftover London broil or grilled strip steak.

MAKES 4 TO 6 SERVINGS

1. Combine the mustard, red wine, garlic, parsley, salt, and pepper in a gallon-size zipper-lock bag. Add the steaks, squeeze out excess air and seal the bag. Massage the marinade into the meat briefly and refrigerate for 4 to 6 hours. Remove from the refrigerator an hour before grilling.

2. Meanwhile, make the salad dressing by mixing the mustard, red wine vinegar, salt and pepper in a large mixing bowl. Whisk in the oil in a slow steady stream. Stir in the herbs (reserving a small amount for garnish). Toss in the tomatoes and scallions and set aside until ready to compose dishes.

3. Preheat grill to medium-high heat; brush grill grate with a wire brush and rub the clean grate liberally with oil. Grill the steaks until browned on the surface and slightly charred at the edges. An instant-read thermometer inserted into the side of the thickest steak should read 130°F for medium-rare results. This will take 4 to 5 minutes per side. Allow steaks to rest for 5 to 10 minutes, loosely covered, before serving. Alternatively, steaks may be pan-sautéed or broiled.

4. Toss salad greens with vinaigrette, tomatoes and scallions. Place a serving of salad on the center of each plate. Thinly slice steaks against the grain, lay slices decoratively over salads and serve.

PORK LOIN ROASTED WITH APRICOT, GARLIC AND SOY

When I was growing up in suburban USA, my mom (and thousands of other moms) made this recipe (and dozens of variations with chicken, meatballs, shrimp, you name it). What wasn't to love? It was sweet (apricot preserves), salty (soy sauce), and pungent (garlic). But it was also something we didn't have a name for at the time—umami—the savory flavor of roasted meat, mushrooms, and above all else, soy sauce. Asian cultures knew all about umami, but American flavor experts denied its existence at the time. Moms are so hip.

1 **bone-in pork loin roast, between 3 and 4 pounds**

Sea salt and freshly ground pepper

1 **jar (8 oz) apricot preserves**

3 **garlic cloves, finely chopped**

½ **cup soy sauce**

MAKES 4 SERVINGS

1. Preheat oven to 375°F. Season the pork generously with salt and pepper and put it on a rack in a roasting pan; set aside.

2. Mix the preserves, garlic and soy sauce in a medium mixing bowl until well combined. Spoon preserves mixture over the meat. Roast the pork until golden brown and an instant read thermometer inserted in the center reads 145°F, about 1 hour. Baste with drippings twice during the last half hour of roasting.

3. Remove roast from oven and rest for 10 to 15 minutes, covered loosely with foil. Slice and serve immediately. Roast is also delicious sliced cold as leftovers.

PORK CHOPS WITH PORT WINE, CRANBERRIES AND THYME

Pork loin chops are quick and simple, tender, flavorful and juicy, which is why I rely on them as a mainstay quick dinner. Although this recipe is super fast and easy, making it the perfect weeknight family's-got-to-eat-now kind of recipe, it is also surprisingly elegant, which lets you serve it for company you want to impress. I guess that makes it perfect any time. I've found that the secret to success with pork chops is allowing the meat to rest for a few minutes before serving.

4   boneless pork loin chops
    (4 to 5 ounces each), about
    ¾ inch thick

    Sea salt and freshly ground
    black pepper

½   cup all-purpose flour

1   tablespoon extra virgin olive oil

3   tablespoons unsalted butter

1   large shallot, finely chopped

1   cup port wine

½   cup dried cranberries

2   teaspoons minced fresh thyme
    leaves plus thyme sprigs
    for garnish

1   cup chicken broth

MAKES 4 SERVINGS

1. Season the pork chops liberally with salt and pepper. Put flour on a large platter or on a sheet of foil and season liberally with salt and pepper. Heat oil and 1 tablespoon of butter in a large heavy frying pan over medium heat until oil is shimmering.

2. Dredge the pork chops in flour, patting off any excess. Sauté the pork chops until golden brown on both sides, about 3 minutes per side. Remove from pan and set chops aside on a plate; loosely cover with foil.

3. Return the pan to the heat. Add shallot and sauté until softened, 1 to 2 minutes. Add port wine, cranberries and thyme. Increase heat to medium-high and reduce liquid by half, scraping pan bottom with a wooden spoon to loosen browned bits, 3 to 5 minutes.

4. Increase heat to high; add broth and any accumulated meat juices from the meat plate; boil until liquid reduces and thickens slightly, about 3 minutes. Add salt and pepper to taste.

5. Reduce heat to medium; return pork to pan, turning meat in the sauce to coat. Simmer to heat pork through and blend flavors, about 3 minutes. Transfer pork to a serving plate and set aside for 2 minutes. Meanwhile, reduce heat to low and swirl remaining 2 tablespoons of butter in the pan until melted and incorporated, thickening the sauce. Spoon sauce over meat and serve immediately.

OVEN-BAKED SPARERIBS

Though **BBQ'd** ribs are closely associated with summertime grilling, this recipe is welcome any time. In fact it's perfect for those cold wintery months since it can be completely prepared indoors and produces fall-off-the-bone tender ribs. If you like and have an outdoor grill nearby, finish the ribs on the grill instead of in the broiler.

1   teaspoon garlic powder

1   teaspoon ground black pepper

1   tablespoon chili powder

1   teaspoon celery salt

1   teaspoon ground cumin

1   teaspoon paprika

1   teaspoon sugar

1   teaspoon sea salt

2   racks pork spareribs

2   cups of your favorite jarred
    bar-b-que sauce
    (For supermarket brands,
    I like Bull's Eye or KC Masterpiece)

MAKES 4 SERVINGS

1. Mix garlic powder, pepper, chili powder, celery salt, cumin, paprika, sugar and salt in a small bowl. Rub the ribs with the spices on both sides, wrap in plastic and refrigerate for at least 2 hours or up to 24 hours.

2. Preheat oven to 350°F. Place ribs in a single layer on a rack in a roasting pan with 3 inches of water in the bottom of pan. If necessary, use 2 pans. Cover the pan(s) tightly with foil. Bake ribs until your house smells wonderful and a knife can be inserted easily into the meat, about 1½ hours. When checking doneness, remove the foil from pan carefully (as steam will escape). Ribs may be made ahead until this point, cooled, rewrapped carefully in foil and refrigerated, proceeding with the next step when ready to finish cooking ribs.

3. Preheat broiler. Drain any liquid from pan. Put the ribs in a single layer on a broiler pan and brush liberally (all over) with bar-b-que sauce. Place under broiler to brown, watching carefully that the ribs do not burn. Serve immediately with extra bbq sauce.

RACK OF LAMB WITH GARLIC AND MINT CRUST

My grandmother always served lamb chops with mint jelly. Lamb and mint are natural partners, but the sugar, I can do without. This recipe honors the lamb-mint tradition but by switching to fresh mint in a crackling crust and a rack of lamb rather than individual chops, the whole dish upgrades to first class. Each rack of lamb is composed of seven or eight small rib lamb chops and serves two people. It roasts in less than half an hour and makes a beautiful presentation. Racks are easy to cut into chops, so feel free to show off and carve at the table.

3 garlic cloves, peeled, cut in a few chunks

1 cup (packed) fresh mint leaves

¼ cup (packed) flat-leaf parsley leaves

1 bunch fresh chives, coarsely chopped

2 teaspoons coarsely ground black pepper

1 teaspoon sea salt

¼ cup plus 2 tablespoons extra virgin olive oil

3 cups fresh breadcrumbs

3 racks of lamb (each with 7 or 8 bones), well trimmed, frenched (see note)

3 tablespoons Dijon mustard

MAKES 6 SERVINGS

1. To make the herb crust, combine the garlic, mint, parsley, chives, salt, pepper, and ¼ cup of oil in a food processor fitted with the steel blade. Process in pulses until everything is uniformly finely chopped. Add the breadcrumbs and process until all ingredients are well combined. Crumbs should be moist but not too wet. (Can be prepared in the morning and refrigerated in a zipper-lock bag.)

2. Take the lamb out of the refrigerator an hour before cooking to allow it to lose its chill. Preheat oven to 400°F.

3. Sprinkle each lamb rack generously with salt and pepper, rubbing into meat all over. Heat the remaining 2 tablespoons oil in a large, heavy, ovenproof frying pan (cast iron works well) over medium-high heat. Brown the lamb racks on both sides in the hot oil (you will probably need to do one at a time). Allow lamb to rest for 10 to 20 minutes, until cool to touch.

4. Spread each cooled rack of lamb with Dijon mustard to help the breadcrumb mixture to adhere. Firmly press the breadcrumb/herb mixture onto the racks in an even coat. Put bone side down on a sheet pan and roast until a meat thermometer inserted into center of lamb registers 130°f for rare to medium-rare, about 25 minutes. Let stand for 10 minutes before carving into chops. Serve sliced or as whole racks and carve into chops at the table.

❋ NOTE: A frenched rack has the bones cleaned of meat, fat and sinew so that the chops can be neatly picked up for eating. Depending on how you want the rack cleaned, the bone can be exposed completely up to the eye of the meat or just a few inches at the end.

FRESH BREADCRUMBS

Making fresh breadcrumbs is a snap, takes only a few minutes and the results are so worth it. Simply tear apart a small italian roll or baguette into large pieces, drop into a food processor fitted with the steel blade and process until the bread is in crumbs. Extra breadcrumbs can even be frozen in a zipper-lock bag for future use.

HOPE'S VEAL LOAF (BY WAY OF CAROLINA'S)

In the 1980s, near the Rittenhouse Square section of Philadelphia, there stood a restaurant by the name of Carolina's that was a hip neighborhood bistro with exceptional food and a great bar. Their veal loaf inspired me. It was lighter and more flavorful than the meatloaf I grew up with. Part of the reason was the more delicate flavor and smoother texture of ground veal, but the switch from sweet tangy ketchup to Dijon mustard, and flip-flopping Italian seasoning with lemon and herbes de Provence were real game changers—Mom's meatloaf after a day at the spa!

2	large or extra large eggs, beaten
2	garlic cloves, pressed or minced
1	cup plain fresh breadcrumbs
	Juice of ½ lemon
2	tablespoons Dijon mustard
2	teaspoons dried herbes de Provence
1½	lbs ground veal
2	teaspoons sea salt, plus more to taste
1	teaspoon freshly ground black pepper, plus more to taste

MAKES 4 SERVINGS

1. Preheat oven to 350°F.

2. Mix the eggs, garlic, breadcrumbs, lemon juice, mustard and herbs in a large mixing bowl. Add the veal and 1 teaspoon each of salt and pepper, and mix everything together with your hands. Form mixture into a rectangular loaf shape on a rimmed sheet pan lined with foil or in a nonstick loaf pan. Season the surface of loaf with additional salt and pepper.

3. Bake until the loaf feels firm and an instant-read thermometer inserted in the center reads 155°F, about 1 hour. Remove from the oven and let rest for 5 to 10 minutes. Slice and serve.

SAUTÉED CHICKEN PROVENÇAL

Fresh and simple, fragrant with good olive oil, sweet peppers, tomatoes, olives, and fennel; when you want to drift dreamily, dream Provençal dreams! This dish glows with the unfiltered sunshine of southern France. It takes about 15 minutes of active work, and then you're off duty while the chicken spits lazily on a low burner, drifting to doneness.

¼ cup all-purpose flour

Sea salt and freshly ground black pepper

8 chicken thighs or a combination of thighs and legs

3 tablespoons extra virgin olive oil

1 onion, thinly sliced

½ red bell pepper, stemmed, seeded and sliced

½ small fennel bulb, trimmed, thinly sliced, reserving a few sprigs of the feathery fronds for garnish

2 garlic cloves, minced

3 ripe plum tomatoes, cored and coarsely chopped (use drained Italian canned, if not in season)

½ cup pitted black niçoise olives

½ cup dry white wine

3 tablespoons chopped flat-leaf parsley

MAKES 4 SERVINGS

1. Season flour with plenty of salt and pepper on a large plate or piece of foil. Dredge chicken in the flour mixture, coating it well and patting off excess.

2. Heat 2 tablespoons of the oil in a large frying pan over medium-high heat. Sauté the chicken on both sides until lightly golden, about 5 minutes per side. Remove chicken from the pan and put on a plate.

3. Return the pan to the stove and reduce the heat to medium. Add the remaining oil and sauté onion, pepper and fennel until tender, about 5 minutes. Add the garlic and sauté until aromatic, about 30 seconds. Increase heat to medium-high, add tomatoes and olives and cook until tomatoes start to break down, about 8 minutes, stirring as needed.

4. Add white wine and cook until the wine evaporates and sauce thickens slightly, about 5 more minutes. Add parsley, reserved fennel fronds, salt, pepper and any juices which have accumulated under the chicken to the pan. Reduce heat to medium-low, add the chicken, cover and cook in the sauce until the chicken is cooked through, about 20 minutes.

5. Transfer the chicken to a warm serving platter and pour the sauce over. Garnish with additional parsley, if desired.

CHICKEN BREASTS WITH LEMON AND WHITE WINE

Chicken piccata is one of the old-school Italian restaurant dishes that I grew up eating in the small family-style restaurants found in South Philly, always accompanied by dense, crusty bread and a bowl of spaghetti marinara—my idea of soul food.

¼ cup all-purpose flour

1 teaspoon sea salt, plus more to taste

1 teaspoon freshly ground black pepper, plus more to taste

4 boneless chicken breast halves, pounded to about 1½ inches thick

1 tablespoon extra virgin olive oil

4 tablespoons unsalted butter

2 shallots, peeled and finely chopped

½ cup dry white wine

Juice of 1 lemon

1 cup chicken broth

3 tablespoons chopped flat-leaf parsley

½ lemon, thinly sliced

MAKES 4 SERVINGS

1. Season flour with salt and pepper on a large plate or piece of foil. Dredge chicken in the flour mixture, coating it well and patting off excess.

2. Heat oil and 1 tablespoon of the butter in a large frying pan over medium-high heat. When the butter foam subsides, sauté the chicken on both sides until lightly golden, about 3 minutes per side. Remove chicken from the pan and put on a plate.

3. Return the pan to the stove and reduce the heat to medium. Add 1 tablespoon butter to pan and sauté shallots until softened, 1 to 2 minutes. Increase heat to medium-high, add the wine and deglaze by scraping all of the brown bits from bottom of pan. Boil for a few minutes to evaporate alcohol. Add lemon juice and chicken broth. Add parsley and any accumulated juices from the chicken, and thicken the sauce slightly by reducing it over medium-high heat for several minutes.

4. Reduce heat to low and add remaining butter, swirling the pan until the butter melts. Do not allow to boil! Taste sauce for seasoning, adding salt or pepper if necessary.

5. Add chicken to the skillet with the sauce and continue simmering, turning the filets over in the sauce two or three times to coat with sauce. Transfer the chicken to a warm serving platter and pour the sauce on top. Garnish with lemon slices and additional parsley. Serve immediately.

SUMMER CHICKEN SALAD

Summer salads are always popular and oh so easy to put together with the bounty of fresh produce available. This particular salad was born from a chilled, leftover rotisserie chicken and a cooked ear of corn that were taking up space in my refrigerator. I bathed them in a lemony fresh vinaigrette and voila!

1   cooked chicken, rotisserie or oven roasted, cooled

2   ripe Hass avocados, peeled, seeded and diced in large cubes

2   large ripe tomatoes, diced in large cubes

1   ear cooked corn, cooled, kernals cut off of cob

2   large handfuls of baby arugula, washed and dried

1   teaspoon sea salt

1   teaspoon freshly ground black pepper

    Juice of 1 lemon

3   tablespoons extra virgin olive oil

2   tablespoons capers in brine, drained

2   tablespoons chopped fresh chives

MAKES 4 TO 6 SERVINGS

1. Remove the skin from the chicken and discard. Remove the bones and cut meat into bite-size pieces. Toss the chicken meat, avocados, tomatoes, corn and arugula in a large salad bowl.

2. Add salt, pepper, lemon juice and olive oil and toss to mix. Add capers and chives, mix and taste for seasoning, adding more salt and pepper if necessary. Serve immediately.

GRILLED GREEK ISLAND CHICKEN

¼ cup extra virgin olive oil

2 tablespoons fresh lemon juice

2 garlic cloves, smashed

2 tablespoons chopped mint

Coarse sea salt and freshly ground black pepper

4 boneless chicken breast halves, pounded to about ¾ inch thick

SALAD

1 garlic clove, minced

1 tablespoons fresh oregano, chopped

2 tablespoons extra virgin olive oil

1 tablespoon red wine vinegar

2 red ripe tomatoes, cored and finely chopped

½ English cucumber, peeled, seeded and finely chopped

2 tablespoons finely chopped sweet onion (such as Vidalia)

3 tablespoons small capers in brine, drained

Sea salt and freshly ground black pepper

½ cup crumbled Greek feta cheese

1 tablespoon chopped herbs, such as flat-leaf parsley and/or mint

This recipe combines a rustic Greek salad with juicy grilled chicken breasts. Greek island cuisine often pairs garlic with the mint that grows wild in abundance over the hillsides. Perfect in summer, when tomatoes are at their peak, serve this dish al fresco as part of a Mediterranean island–style buffet.

MAKES 4 SERVINGS

1. Mix the olive oil, lemon juice, garlic, mint, salt, and pepper in a gallon-size zipper-lock bag. Add the chicken, squeeze out excess air, and seal. Refrigerate about 1 hour.

2. Mix the garlic, oregano, olive oil, and vinegar in a medium mixing bowl. Add the tomatoes, cucumber, onion and capers, and toss everything together. Season with salt and pepper. The salad may be made up to 6 hours ahead and refrigerated, but let it sit at room temperature for at least 30 minutes before finishing.

3. Preheat grill to high heat; brush grill grate with a wire brush and rub the clean grate liberally with oil. Grill the chicken until lightly browned on the surface and resilient to the touch. An instant-read thermometer inserted into the side of the thickest chicken breast should read 160°F. This will take 2 to 3 minutes per side.

4. Arrange chicken on a serving platter. Toss the cheese and herbs with the salad and mound on top of the chicken. Serve immediately.

BRAISED MOROCCAN CHICKEN

Breathe. Can you smell the cinnamon, cumin and bay; the sweet flesh of simmering dried plums, apricots, and tomato; the pungent fumes from garlic, green olives, and black pepper? If you have any doubts about where you're going, your nose knows. You're Morocco bound. These spicy, sweet and salty flavors are synonymous with North Africa, where tagine-style braised dishes are served family-style, heaped on a bed of couscous.

8   bone-in chicken legs and thighs

Sea salt and freshly ground black pepper

¼   teaspoons ground cinnamon

¼   teaspoons ground cumin

3   tablespoons olive oil

1   yellow onion, thinly sliced

2   garlic cloves, chopped

6   ripe plum tomatoes, cored and coarsely chopped (use drained Italian canned, if not in season)

1   cup pitted green olives

1   tablespoon tomato paste

Juice of 1 orange

1   cup chicken broth

½   cup pitted prunes

½   cup dried pitted apricots

1   bay leaf

3   tablespoons chopped flat-leaf parsley

MAKES 4 SERVINGS

1. Season the chicken with salt, pepper, cinnamon, and cumin on both sides.

2. Heat 2 tablespoons of the oil in a deep heavy frying pan over medium-high heat. Sauté the chicken just until browned, 3 to 4 minutes per side. Remove chicken from pan and set aside on a plate.

3. Add the remaining oil to pan, and sauté onion until translucent, about 2 minutes. Add the garlic and sauté just until aromatic, about 30 seconds. Add the tomatoes, olives, tomato paste, orange juice, chicken broth, prunes, apricots and bay leaf and bring to a simmer, stirring as needed.

4. Add the reserved chicken and any accumulated juices to the pan, spooning sauce over chicken. Cover and braise on a low simmer until chicken is tender and cooked through, about 30 minutes.

5. Remove the bay leaf, garnish with parsley and serve.

FISH + SHELLFISH

GINGER AND SOY GRILLED SALMON

The pervasive richness of Alaskan king salmon makes it brown beautifully and retain its moisture even when the fish, is exposed to incendiary heat, all of which means it is fated for grilling. Kekap manis, the sweet soy sauce from Indonesia that tops this fish, is worth seeking out at Asian markets. It has the same savory fermented quality of Japanese soy sauce, but it is darker and treacle-thick from a hefty dose of palm sugar, a natural sweetener known for its low glycemic index.

½ cup soy sauce

2 tablespoons peeled, grated gingerroot

3 scallions, roots trimmed, sliced in half lengthwise

2 or 3 garlic cloves, peeled and smashed

¼ teaspoon sesame oil

4 pieces salmon fillet (6 ounces each), skin on

2 tablespoons mild vegetable oil for brushing salmon

1 to 2 tablespoons kekap manis (sweet soy sauce), for garnish

2 tablespoons thinly sliced scallions, for garnish

MAKES 4 SERVINGS

1. Mix soy sauce, ginger, halved scallions, garlic and sesame oil in a rectangular glass baking dish. Put salmon in marinade and turn to coat evenly. Refrigerate for 1 hour.

2. Preheat grill to high. Brush grill grate with a wire brush and rub the clean grate liberally with oil.

3. Remove salmon from marinade and dry with paper towels, removing any pieces of ginger or garlic clinging to the fish. Brush fish with a light coating of oil and grill until the fish feels firm and starts to flake when gently prodded, about 4 minutes per side. Do not overcook; the fish should still be translucent in the center when it is done.

4. Carefully remove fish from grill, (skin will be crispy) and arrange on a serving platter. Garnish decoratively with kekap manis and thinly sliced scallions. Serve immediately.

WARM SALMON SALAD WITH SPINACH, ORANGE AND LEMON SOY VINAIGRETTE

2 tablespoons soy sauce

Zest of ½ orange, finely grated on a Microplane grater

4 pieces salmon fillet (6 ounces each), skin removed

1 tablespoons extra virgin olive oil

Coarse sea salt and freshly ground black pepper

2 tablespoons toasted chopped almonds, for garnish

1 bunch chives, coarsely chopped, for garnish

SALAD

1 bag (8 oz) baby spinach

2 navel oranges, peeled and cut into skinless segments

Fine sea salt and freshly ground black pepper

1 tablespoon soy sauce

Juice of 1 lemon

3 tablespoons extra virgin olive oil

This marriage of perfectly grilled salmon, aromatic from a marinade of soy and orange zest, paired with a crisp, earthy, cool spinach salad jeweled by bits of orange segment is one of the simplest pleasures you can attain on a summer evening. It looks and tastes impressively complex, but the whole thing takes less than 30 minutes to throw together.

MAKES 4 SERVINGS

1. Preheat oven to 400°F.

2. Combine soy sauce and orange zest in a small bowl. Brush salmon with soy mixture, drizzle with oil, seasoning well with salt and pepper and set aside on an oiled sheet pan for 15 minutes.

3. For the salad combine spinach, oranges, salt and pepper in a large bowl and toss to combine.

4. Mix the soy sauce, lemon juice, and oil in a small bowl with a whisk. Taste for seasoning adding additional salt and pepper, if needed.

5. Roast the salmon until the fish feels firm and starts to flake when gently prodded, about 8 minutes. Do not overcook; the fish should still be translucent in the center when it is done. Transfer salmon to a platter; blot with paper towels if needed to absorb excess oil.

6. Toss the spinach and oranges with the vinaigrette and make a mound in the center of each plate. Top with salmon filet. Garnish salmon with almonds and decorate plate with chives.

GRILLED SWORDFISH STEAKS WITH MANGO SALSA

Tart, tangy and sweet, mango stars in the cool and flavorful salsa that blankets these savory grilled swordfish steaks. I adore the combination of the warm grilled fish juxtaposed by a gilding of cool raw salsa—tropical paradise!

4 swordfish steaks (about 6 ounces each)

2 tablespoons olive oil, to brush fish

Sea salt and freshly ground black pepper

1 recipe Mango Salsa (page 47)

MAKES 4 SERVINGS

1. Preheat grill to medium-high. Brush grill grate with a wire brush and rub the clean grate liberally with oil.

2. Brush the fish with olive oil and season both sides liberally with salt and pepper.

3. Grill the fish until the flesh feels firm, about 4 minutes per side. Do not overcook; the fish should just have turned opaque in the center when it is done. Remove fish carefully from grill and place on a serving platter. Allow fish to rest for 5 minutes, loosely covered with foil, before serving.

4. Spoon salsa directly onto each steak and serve immediately, passing additional salsa on the side.

RED SNAPPER WITH ARTICHOKES, FETA AND LEMON

The delicate whiter-than-white flaky flesh against the coral skin of red snapper is as gorgeous as it is delicious. In this preparation, I top it with a chunky mix of artichokes, tomato, feta cheese, and herbs. All that's missing is a Greek sunset!

½ cup homemade or purchased mayonnaise, preferably Hellman's

Juice of 1 lemon

1 small garlic clove, minced or pressed

2 tablespoons Greek feta cheese

2 tablespoon freshly grated Parmigiano-Reggiano cheese

½ can (14 oz) artichoke hearts in water, drained and roughly chopped

1 plum tomato, cored and cut in small dice

1 tablespoon finely chopped mint leaves

2 tablespoons finely chopped fresh dill

Coarse sea salt

Freshly ground black pepper

1 tablespoon extra virgin olive oil

4 red snapper fillets (about 6 ounces each, skin on

MAKES 4 SERVINGS

1. Preheat oven to 475°F (really).

2. Mix mayonnaise, 1 tablespoon of the lemon juice, the garlic, feta, Parmigiano, artichoke hearts, tomato, mint and 1 tablespoon of the dill in a small bowl, combining thoroughly. Season to taste salt and pepper to taste, being careful with the salt as feta can be salty.

3. Oil the bottom of a roasting pan with olive oil and place snapper fillets, skin side down in pan. Season fillets liberally with salt, pepper and 1 tablespoon of lemon juice, and rub into the fish. Top each fillet with a generous amount of artichoke mixture, spreading evenly to coat the top of fish.

4. Roast the fish until just cooked through, about 10 minutes. Sprinkle remaining 1 tablespoon of dill onto fillets and serve immediately.

ROASTED WHOLE BRANZINO WITH LEMON AND HERBS

Whole roasted sea bass (*branzino* in Italian) is a dramatic and delicious way to present fresh fish. Dressed simply with lemon, herbs, sea salt, pepper and olive oil, the fish shines as the star of the table! You will need to find a good fishmonger in your area to buy the whole fish. Ask him or her to clean it and scale it for you.

1   black sea bass (branzino), weighing between 2½ and 3 pounds, cleaned and scaled

Coarse sea salt and freshly ground black pepper

2   lemons, 1 halved and 1 sliced into ¼-inch-thick rounds

1   bunch fresh thyme

¼   cup extra virgin olive oil, plus extra for garnish

MAKES 2 SERVINGS

1. Preheat oven to 400°F

2. Salt the fish liberally inside and out. Season more gently with pepper. Put the fish on a rimmed sheet pan lined with foil and squeeze juice of half lemon over top. Put 3 or 4 thyme branches in the cavity of the fish along with 4 slices of lemon. Drizzle the interior of the fish liberally with oil.

3. Remove the leaves from 2 thyme branches and sprinkle over the fish. Lay the remaining lemon slices on top of the fish, you may have only 2 or 3. Season with more salt and pepper and drizzle with more olive oil.

4. Roast until the skin is crisp and the fish flakes to gently pressure when pressed (about 120°F on an instant-read thermometer), about 15 minutes. Remove the sheet pan from the oven, and squeeze the remaining lemon over top; cover the fish loosely with foil and let it rest for 5 minutes.

5. Serve immediately, filleting the fish and serving with the roasted lemon slices and a little additional olive oil, salt and pepper.

SAUTÉED SHRIMP WITH SHERRY AND GARLIC

Sherry, the brandy-fortified white wine of Jerez, Spain, is a complex brew, combining full fruit and savory notes from barrel aging. It enriches the briny freshness of this scampi-like shrimp preparation immeasurably. Be sure to use a good-quality dry Spanish sherry and serve the finished dish with fresh bread for dipping into the sauce.

1 **pound extra large (16–20 count) shrimp, peeled and deveined, with tail on**

2 **tablespoons dry sherry**

 Sea salt and freshly ground black pepper

2 **tablespoons chopped flat-leaf parsley**

2 **tablespoons extra virgin olive oil**

2 **tablespoons unsalted butter**

3 **garlic cloves, finely chopped**

MAKES 4 SERVINGS

1. Toss shrimp, 1 tablespoon sherry, salt and pepper to taste, 1 tablespoon of the parsley and 1 tablespoon of the oil in a glass baking dish or casserole. Cover and marinate on the kitchen counter for 30 minutes.

2. Heat remaining oil and butter in a large sauté pan over medium-high heat. Add shrimp and garlic, and sauté shrimp until the shrimp just begin to firm and become opaque, about 3 minutes.

3. Add the remaining sherry, sautéing for another 30 seconds to evaporate alcohol. Taste for seasoning, sprinkle with remaining parsley and serve immediately.

SQUEEZING CITRUS JUICE

The easiest method to extract the juice from a lemon, lime or grapefruit half is to first roll the fruit around under you palm on the counter for 30 seconds, softening the fruit and allowing the juices to come to the surface. Slice the fruit in half along its equator and place the tines of a dinner fork in the cut side of one half. While you turn the fork, turn and squeeze the fruit, catching the juice in a small bowl.

SHRIMP SALAD WITH LEMON AND DILL

Shrimp salad always makes the occasion feel festive. I am not a lover of mayonnaise, so I tend to use very little and season it heavily with celery salt (for great flavor), lemon and dill. It is very fresh and very simple, improving with flavor when made a day ahead.

1   dozen extra large shrimp (16–20 count)

3   celery ribs, washed and finely diced

Juice of 1 lemon

1   teaspoon celery salt

1   tablespoon chopped fresh dill, plus an additional sprig for garnish

¼   cup homemade or purchased mayonnaise, preferably Hellman's

MAKES 4 TO 6 SERVINGS

1. Bring 2 cups of generously salted water to a boil in a saucepan. Add the shrimp. Stir to disperse, cover and remove from heat. Allow to steep for 5 minutes. Drain, cool, peel, devein and cut into ½-inch pieces.

2. Mix celery, lemon juice, celery salt, dill and mayonnaise in a medium mixing bowl. Add shrimp and toss to coat. Taste for seasoning, adding additional salt, if needed. Serve immediately or refrigerate overnight. Serve garnished with a sprig of dill.

SPANISH RICE WITH SHELLFISH

2   tablespoons extra virgin olive oil

½   small onion, chopped

1   carrot, peeled and chopped

1   celery rib, chopped

1   garlic clove, smashed
    and chopped

1   cup Arborio, Bomba, or other
    medium-short rice

3   plum tomatoes, cored and
    roughly chopped

2   cups chicken broth

½   teaspoon saffron threads

¼   teaspoon *pimentón de la Vera*
    or Spanish paprika (sweet or hot)

    Sea salt and freshly ground
    black pepper

½   can (13.75 oz) quartered
    artichoke hearts, drained

1   dozen little neck clams, rinsed
    and drained

1   cup frozen peas

12 large shrimp, peeled
    and deveined

6   extra-large diver scallops

My rendition of paella is faster (no poultry to cook through), fresher (no chorizo or ham), and simpler (the whole thing takes less than 20 minutes to prepare) than the original, but no less full flavored and delicious. You can use any medium- to short-grain rice, Arborio is probably the easiest to find. Everything cooks together in a large pan in a dazzling, steaming, raucous display of rice, vegetables and shellfish. The flavors sing together; I recommend enjoying with a big, red Spanish wine!

MAKES 6 SERVINGS

1. Heat the olive oil in a large heavy saucepan or frying pan over medium heat. Add the onion, carrot and celery and sauté until the onion is translucent, about 5 minutes. Add the garlic and rice and sauté for 1 to 2 minutes until well coated with oil and fragrant.

2. Add tomatoes, broth, saffron, paprika and salt and pepper to taste. Stir well and bring to a simmer.

3. Add artichokes and clams, nestling the clams into the rice mixture. Cover and cook until at least half the clams have opened, approximately 10 minutes.

4. Add peas, shrimp, and scallops and continue to cook until all the clams have opened and the shrimp and scallops are firm to the touch, about 5 more minutes. Remove from heat, cover the pan with a towel and wait 5 minutes to allow the towel to absorb extra steam that could cause the rice to be mushy.

ODEON'S SAUTÉED CRAB CAKES

Odeon, a wonderful old-style French bistro in Philadelphia, housed in a 19th century bookshop, is now defunct, but their crab cakes live on my memory, and now on these pages. The bigger the lumps of crab, the better the cakes will be.

1   pound lump or jumbo lump crabmeat

¼   cup finely chopped flat-leaf parsley

1   bunch scallions, roots trimmed, thinly sliced

¾   cup fresh breadcrumbs

2   large eggs

¼   cup milk

    Pinch of cayenne pepper

1   teaspoon Worcestershire sauce

    Fine sea salt and freshly ground black pepper

3   tablespoons unsalted butter

1   lemon, thinly sliced, for garnish

    Rémoulade Sauce (page 46), for garnish

MAKES 6 SERVINGS

1. Pick over crabmeat to remove shells, keeping meat as whole as possible. Toss crab with the parsley, scallions and breadcrumbs in a large mixing bowl.

2. Mix eggs, milk, cayenne, Worcestershire and salt and pepper to taste in a small bowl, pour over the crab mixture and mix gently to blend, being careful not to break up the crabmeat. Shape into 6 cakes, pressing gently to help them hold together.

3. Heat the butter over medium heat in a large nonstick frying pan until sizzling. Brown the crab cakes on both sides, about 4 minutes per side. Serve immediately with lemon slices and rémoulade sauce.

CLAMS STEAMED WITH GARLIC AND WHITE WINE

Whenever I prepare this dish, regardless of where I am, immediately I am transported to the seaside. Nothing brings the seashore into your kitchen like steaming clams. The preparation is simple and straightforward. Serve it with crusty bread, a salad and a crisp acidic white wine—the perfect dinner à deux.

½ cup coarse sea salt (for soaking clams)

2 dozen littleneck clams

¼ cup extra virgin olive oil

2 garlic cloves (or more to taste), very thinly sliced

2 cups crisp white wine, such as pinot grigio

¼ cup finely chopped flat-leaf parsley

MAKES 2 SERVINGS

1. Fill a bowl large enough to hold clams with cold water. Add salt and stir to dissolve. Add clams to salt water and soak for about 10 minutes.

2. Meanwhile, heat oil over low heat in a large pot with a lid, add the garlic and sauté just until aromatic, for a few minutes. Add wine and raise heat to medium; bring to a boil.

3. Lift the clams from the salt water carefully, leaving any sediment in the bottom of the bowl. Rinse quickly in cold water. Immediately add to the boiling wine and scatter parsley over top. Cover pot and increase heat to high, steaming clams until they open, 5 to 8 minutes.

4. Serve clams immediately in a large bowl with the steaming broth and some good crusty bread.

DANAI GREEK MUSSELS WITH TOMATO AND FETA

This recipe was inspired by a trip to northern Greece, specifically the beautiful peninsula of Sithonia in the Halkidiki region sometimes referred to as "the Greek Riviera." We were served this delicious combination of mussels, tomato, and feta for lunch in individual casserole dishes. I often serve it with rice and a salad for a light dinner.

¼ cup extra virgin olive oil

4 garlic cloves, chopped

1 cup dry vermouth

3 dozen mussels, cleaned, beards removed

2 tablespoons finely diced red bell pepper

½ can (28 oz) San Marzano tomatoes, drained

Sea salt and freshly ground black pepper

½ cup crumbled good-quality Greek feta cheese

1 tablespoon finely chopped flat-leaf parsley

MAKES 4 SERVINGS

1. Heat half of the olive oil in a large, lidded stockpot over medium heat. Add half of the garlic, and sauté for a minute, until softened. Add the vermouth and increase heat to medium-high; bring to a boil. Add the mussels and cover. Boil until mussels open, 3 to 5 minutes. Remove pan from heat, uncover and immediately remove mussels from pan with a slotted spoon, reserving liquid. Shell mussels, discarding shells and reserving meat. Reserve mussels in a bowl, loosely covered. Strain liquid through moistened cheesecloth and reserve.

2. In a medium sauté pan over medium heat, warm the remaining olive oil and sauté garlic and red pepper until aromatic, about 30 seconds. Add tomatoes, crushing them well with your hands as you add them. Add the reserved strained mussel liquid and salt and pepper to taste. Increase heat to medium-high and cook sauce for about 10 minutes, stirring often, until tomatoes are cooked and the sauce is thickened. Lower the heat to medium-low.

3. Add reserved cooked mussels, feta and parsley. Cook and stir gently until feta starts to soften, about 20 seconds. Taste for seasoning and serve in individual small bowls immediately.

VEGETABLES

GRILLED LEMON ASPARAGUS

Asparagus are reinvented on the grill. What were once mere harbingers of spring become full-fledged meaty morsels after grilling. Serve them hot off the grill, at room temperature or chilled. They are the perfect spring-summer grill dish, and oh so easy! Here's a tip: to trim the hard ends off asparagus, grip the end between your thumb and index finger and bend. The asparagus will naturally snap at its tender sweet spot.

1 **pound medium-thick green asparagus, ends snapped off, rinsed**

2 **tablespoons extra virgin olive oil**

Sea salt and freshly ground black pepper

Finely grated zest of ½ lemon

MAKES 4 SERVINGS

1. Preheat grill to high heat. Brush grill grate with a wire brush and rub the clean grate liberally with oil.

2. Drizzle asparagus with olive oil and toss to coat thoroughly. Season liberally with salt and pepper to taste.

3. Using tongs, place the lengths of asparagus perpendicular to the grill grate to keep them from slipping into the fire. Grill until bright green and slightly charred, 2 to 3 minutes, rolling as needed to keep them cooking evenly.

4. Transfer to serving dish and garnish with lemon zest. Serve immediately or at room temperature.

ZUCCHINI FETA GRATIN

1 tablespoon unsalted butter

1 garlic clove, halved

1 tablespoon extra virgin olive oil

4 medium green zucchini, halved lengthwise, cut in ½-inch slices

1 small yellow onion, diced

Sea salt and freshly ground black pepper

1 garlic clove, finely chopped

1 cup heavy cream

1 large or extra large egg

2 tablespoons chopped fresh dill

1 cup crumbled good-quality feta cheese

½ cup fresh breadcrumbs

1 tablespoon melted unsalted butter

Zucchini is bland, which is both its bane and its saving grace. Bland is boring, but it is also versatile, and zucchini, which is abundant every summer, is nothing if not versatile. This recipe was inspired by my love of Greek flavors and of dishes that can be cooked one day and served the next.

MAKES 6 SERVINGS

1. Preheat oven to 350°F.

2. Rub a 10-inch round gratin dish or glass pie plate with butter and split garlic clove; set aside.

3. Heat oil in a large sauté pan over medium-high heat. Sauté zucchini and onion, seasoning liberally with salt and pepper, until the onion starts to look translucent and the zucchini begins to wilt a bit, about 3 minutes. Add chopped garlic and continue to sauté until aromatic, about another minute. Remove from heat and set aside.

4. Mix the cream, egg and dill together in a large bowl, seasoning with salt and pepper to taste. Combine with zucchini mixture and the feta cheese, and pour into prepared baking dish.

5. Mix breadcrumbs with melted butter and sprinkle over zucchini. Bake uncovered until bubbly and brown, about 45 minutes. Allow to rest for 10 minutes and serve immediately. Or allow to cool, refrigerate and reheat at 325°F until bubbly, about 20 minutes, covered for 15, cover removed for last 5 minutes to crisp breadcrumbs.

CORN AND CHEDDAR PUDDING

This dish is a hybrid of a savory pudding, a crustless quiche, and a soufflé. In study after study, corn is the most popular vegetable after potatoes. The combination of sweet and savory in this one-of-a-kind pudding, paired with the nuttiness of sharp cheddar, is an irresistible winning combination that can be prepared rapidly and does not suffer from using canned or frozen corn in the winter months.

3	tablespoons unsalted butter, melted, plus more for buttering pie plate
2	large eggs
1½	tablespoons sugar
2	tablespoons all-purpose flour
½	teaspoon sea salt
2	cups fresh, frozen, or canned (drained) corn kernels
	Pinch of nutmeg
¼	cup milk
½	cup heavy cream
1	cup shredded sharp cheddar cheese

MAKES 4 TO 6 SERVINGS

1. Preheat oven to 350°F. Butter a 9-inch glass pie plate.

2. Whisk eggs very well in a medium mixing bowl. Add melted butter, sugar, flour and salt and whisk until well combined. Add corn, nutmeg, milk, cream and cheese and stir to combine. Pour into the baking dish and bake until the center is set and a knife inserted in the center comes out clean, about 45 minutes.

3. Cool for 10 minutes before serving. Serve hot.

CORN AND CILANTRO SAUTÉ

Corn and cilantro are Mexican plate mates teamed together in countless traditional dishes. In this simple sauté I emphasize their compatibility with an acidic kick of lime and a bit of Serrano pepper heat. I love to use a heavy cast-iron pan for this dish. It sears and caramelizes the sugars in the corn as they turn a nutty shade of brown. Serve this dish with grilled steak and a simple tomato salad for the perfect summer dinner. If you crave the flavors of summer in off months, you can use drained canned corn as a substitute, not perfect, but perfectly adequate.

1   tablespoon extra virgin olive oil

4   ears fresh corn, husked, silk removed, and kernels cut off

½   serrano chile, stemmed, seeded, and minced

1   scallion, roots trimmed, sliced

½   cup chopped fresh cilantro

    Sea salt and freshly ground black pepper

    Juice of 1 lime

MAKES 4 SERVINGS

1. Heat the oil in a large heavy frying pan, preferably cast iron, over medium-high heat. Add corn kernels, serrano chile, scallion, and cilantro, seasoning with salt and pepper to taste. Stir often so that corn does not burn. Cook until the corn starts to blister and color, about 8 minutes.

2. Taste for seasoning, adding additional salt if necessary. Add lime juice and serve immediately.

.

ROASTED TOMATOES

Roasting brings out the natural sweetness of plum tomatoes. Pair them with fresh herbs and a splatter of extra virgin olive oil, then sit back and smile. We love these as a side dish served warm, but also at room temperature or cold. They are perfect on a sandwich, as part of a buffet or served with soft cheeses such as ricotta or chèvre.

6   ripe plum tomatoes, cored and halved lengthwise

Sea salt and freshly ground black pepper

6   fresh thyme sprigs

3   tablespoons extra virgin olive oil

MAKES 4 SERVINGS

1. Preheat oven to 375°F. Line a roasting pan with foil.

2. Put the tomatoes, skin side down, in the roasting pan. Sprinkle liberally with salt and pepper to taste. Lay the whole thyme springs across the tomatoes, and drizzle everything with olive oil. Roast until tomatoes start to collapse and color, about 45 minutes.

3. Serve immediately or reserve and serve at room temperature. Tomatoes may be stored for 3 to 4 days in an airtight container in the refrigerator and used cold.

SPINACH WITH GARLIC, RAISINS AND PINE NUTS

Sicily is as close to North Africa as it is to Italy, so it is natural that its food is a blend of Arabic and European influences. The ingredients in this simple Sicilian spinach sauté—garlic, raisins and pine nuts—leans towards Arabic. Serve it as your green vegetable with roasted meats or chicken for a sweet and savory twist.

½ cup seedless raisins

2 packages (10 oz each) fresh spinach or 4 bunches fresh spinach

2 tablespoons extra virgin olive oil

2 garlic cloves, finely chopped

½ cup toasted pine nuts

Sea salt and freshly ground black pepper

MAKES 4 SERVINGS

1. Put the raisins in a bowl. Cover with boiling water and set aside to plump for 10 minutes; drain.

2. Meanwhile, wash spinach thoroughly in several changes of water, drain well.

3. Heat olive oil in a large frying pan over medium heat. Add garlic and sauté until slightly golden, about 1 minute. Add spinach, raisins, salt and pepper and sauté until spinach is wilted, about 3 minutes. Add pine nuts, toss and taste for seasoning, adding additional salt and pepper if necessary. Serve immediately or may be served at room temperature.

BRAISED STRING BEANS WITH GARLIC

Braised string beans (blanched for tenderness and sautéed for flavor) are a favorite in our house. Add as much garlic as you like and be sure to taste for seasoning as you cook them—beans absorb a lot of salt. If you want, you can omit the butter, although it does add great flavor. Simple and simply delicious.

1 pound green beans, trimmed and washed

1 teaspoon fine sea salt, plus more to taste

1 tablespoon extra-virgin olive oil

1 tablespoon unsalted butter

2 large garlic cloves, roughly chopped

Freshly ground black pepper

MAKES 4 SERVINGS

1. Put the beans in a large saucepan, cover with water and add 1 teaspoon salt. Cover the pot and bring to a boil over high heat. Cook until just starting to become tender, about 5 minutes. Drain.

2. Dry pan and return to medium heat. Add oil and butter and sauté garlic until aromatic, about 1 minute. Add beans to the pan with ½ cup water and continue to cook, tossing often (I use tongs) until beans are tender, 5 to 10 minutes more, depending on how tender you like them. Add additional salt to taste. Pour off excess water. Taste once more for seasoning.

BRAISED ORANGE CARROTS

Carrots, like all root vegetables, are a storehouse of sweetness, but they can become woody and dense as they mature so it is important for a dish like this, where carrots are the star, to choose slender young specimens. Orange and carrots are a winning flavor combination and with the addition of some salt, pepper, and fresh green flat-leaf parsley the flavors sing.

2 tablespoons unsalted butter

1 shallot, peeled, trimmed, and finely chopped

1 bunch carrots (about 6), trimmed, peeled and sliced into ¾-inch-thick slices

1 teaspoon sugar

1 cup freshly squeezed orange juice

Good pinch of sea salt

Freshly ground black pepper

½ cup chopped flat-leaf parsley

MAKES 4 SERVINGS

1. Melt butter in heavy saucepan over medium heat. Add shallot and sauté until translucent (not browned), about 3 minutes.

2. Add carrots and sugar, tossing to coat, and cook for a few minutes until sugar dissolves and starts to glaze carrots, stirring frequently.

3. Add orange juice, salt, pepper and chopped parsley (reserving 2 tablespoons for garnish). Raise heat to medium-high, cover the pan and cook until carrots are tender and nicely glazed, about 10 minutes. The carrots should have absorbed most of the liquid; if necessary, increase heat to high and boil uncovered for several minutes until carrots are glazed but not dry. Garnish with reserved parsley and serve immediately.

POTATO ONION SAUTÉ

I hesitate to share the fact that I love canned potatoes for certain applications, but when I realize that they are nothing more nor less than boiled potatoes, ready for sautéing into hash browns, my culinary cringing subsides. This is my old home fried potato recipe. Fabulous with eggs on a Sunday morning! I use lots of black pepper for a spicy kick.

2 tablespoons extra virgin olive oil

2 cans (14.5 oz each) sliced white potatoes, drained and dried thoroughly

1 yellow onion, thinly sliced

Sea salt and freshly ground black pepper

Lots of sweet paprika

MAKES 4 SERVINGS

1. Heat the oil in a large heavy frying pan over medium-high heat. Add the potatoes and spread out in a single layer as much as possible (you will need to overlap some). Scatter the onion slices over potatoes and season liberally with salt, pepper, and lots of paprika, all to taste. The potatoes should have a light coating of red from the paprika, all over.

2. After about 5 minutes, carefully scrape the bottom layer of potatoes with a spatula and flip. Season again, as above.

3. Repeat step 2 above several times, until potatoes take on a deep brown color and start to look crispy, 20 to 25 minutes. Watch potatoes carefully, adjusting heat so that they do not burn, although there will be a few onions that get nice, crispy and dark. Serve immediately to insure crispness.

POTATO GRATIN

This recipe is one of my oldest and most treasured. Classically French, the combination of garlic, cream and potatoes crowned with nutty Gruyère cheese is mouthwatering. The dish gets brown and crispy ("gratin" comes from the French *grater*, "to scrape"), referring to the brown bits that form on the bottom and sides of the cooking vessel. To insure even cooking, it is important that the potatoes are sliced as thinly and evenly as possible. It is easiest to use a mandoline, a manual slicing machine that used to be the province of professional chefs, but is now widely available to home cooks.

4   large baking potatoes

1   garlic clove, smashed and peeled

1   tablespoon unsalted butter

2   cups grated good-quality Gruyère cheese

Freshly grated nutmeg

Sea salt and freshly ground black pepper

1½ cups heavy cream

MAKES 6 SERVINGS

1. Preheat oven to 350°F.

2. Peel the potatoes, putting the peeled potatoes immediately in a bowl of cold water to prevent oxidation (browning). When all of the potatoes are peeled, drain them, pat them dry and slice into ⅛-inch thick rounds (it's easiest to use a mandoline). Dry potato slices well.

3. Rub a 10-inch round gratin dish or glass pie plate with garlic and butter. Make a layer of potato slices in a circular pattern, covering the bottom of dish, sprinkle the layer with salt, pepper and nutmeg, and cover with ¼ of cheese. Repeat with remaining ingredients 3 times, ending with cheese.

4. Pour cream over potato/cheese mixture. Bake uncovered until bubbly and brown, about 1 hour. Allow to rest, covered loosely, for at least 10 minutes before serving, and serve immediately. Or refrigerate and reheat at 325°F until hot and bubbly, about 25 minutes.

MAPLE-GLAZED ACORN SQUASH

This simple vegetable dish is autumn on a plate. The sugars in the squash caramelize, creating deep earthy flavors, and the maple syrup sets into a candy-like coating. It is delicious directly out of the oven, but equally divine cold the next day!

1 acorn squash, washed, cut in eighths, seeds removed

2 tablespoons extra virgin olive oil

   Sea salt and freshly ground black pepper

½ cup pure maple syrup

MAKES 4 SERVINGS

1. Preheat oven to 400°F. Line a rimmed sheet pan with foil.

2. Toss squash pieces in oil and put on pan skin side down; don't worry if some fall on their sides. Sprinkle liberally with salt and pepper. Roast until tender and starting to brown, about 20 minutes.

3. Pour maple syrup over squash, coating well, and continue to roast, brushing squash with the maple syrup several times, until everything is glazed and bronzed, 5 to 10 minutes more. Transfer to serving dish and serve immediately.

CURRIED CAULIFLOWER

I love the simplicity of roasting vegetables. High heat caramelizes their natural sweetness, and water loss concentrates their savory elements and makes their vegetal flesh turn towards carnal. The curry paste that starts off this recipe makes twice as much as you'll need. This is intentional. It is far more flavorful than dried curry powder, and having a backup in the fridge provides instant pizzazz to grilled chicken, broiled fish, or sautéed greens.

4   teaspoons cumin seeds

2   teaspoon coriander seeds

4   garlic cloves, coarsely chopped

1   piece gingerroot about 4 inches long, peeled and coarsely chopped

1   teaspoon cayenne pepper

2   teaspoons garam masala or curry powder

2   teaspoons sea salt

6   tablespoons olive oil

¼   cup tomato paste

1   or 2 fresh serrano or jalapeño chiles, to taste, stemmed, seeded, and coarsely chopped

1   large bunch fresh cilantro

2   tablespoons water

    Vegetable oil for coating sheet pan

1   head cauliflower, washed, trimmed and separated into small florets

MAKES 4 SERVINGS

1. To make the curry paste: heat a heavy skillet, preferably cast iron, over medium-high heat until very hot, about 5 minutes. Add the cumin and coriander seeds and stir until fragrant and toasted, about 1 minute. Remove from the pan and grind fine with a mortar and pestle or in a coffee grinder.

2. Combine the ground spices, garlic, ginger, cayenne, garam masala, salt, olive oil, tomato paste, chilies, cilantro and water in a food processor equipped with a steel blade, and process into a paste. Reserve half of the curry paste in a covered container in the refrigerator for future use. It will keep about a month.

3. Preheat the oven to 375°F. Line a rimmed sheet pan with foil and coat with oil. Combine the cauliflower in a large bowl with the remaining half of the curry paste and toss until all of the cauliflower is well coated. Scrape onto the sheet pan and roast until the edges of the cauliflower brown, the florets are fork tender, and your house smells delicious, about 25 minutes. Serve immediately or cool to room temperature. (I even like it cold the next day).

CELERY ROOT PUREE

Celery root is a favorite vegetable of the French, traditionally served raw in rémoulade or pureed in a vichyssoise type of soup. I love the pale color, intense celery flavor and silky texture when paired with potatoes in this delicious puree.

2 large celery roots (celeriac), peeled and cut into large chunks

2 round red-skinned or golden potatoes, peeled and cut into large chunks

3 cups whole milk

Sea salt and freshly ground black pepper

MAKES 4 SERVINGS

1. Put celery root, potatoes, milk, salt and pepper in a large saucepan, bring to a simmer over medium heat and cook until vegetables are fork tender, 15 to 20 minutes.

2. Drain vegetables, reserving milk, and puree in a blender or food processor until a smooth puree, adding reserved milk to thin to desired consistency. Adjust seasoning, and serve immediately.

CIPOLLINI ONIONS BRAISED WITH ORANGE AND SHERRY VINEGAR

Cipolini are variety of baby Italian onion. Sugary sweet, these onions have a slight crunch that instantly melts in your mouth. In this recipe I balance their delicate pungency with a hint of orange and the sweet acidity of sherry vinegar. Their season is relatively short, but they are well worth seeking out while available. I especially like to serve this dish around the holidays.

1 pound cipolini onions, whole, unpeeled

2 tablespoons extra virgin olive oil

1 tablespoon sugar

Sea salt and freshly ground black pepper

¼ cup sherry vinegar

Juice of 1 large orange

½ cup water

2 tablespoons chopped flat-leaf parsley, for garnish

MAKES 4 SERVINGS

1. Preheat oven to 375°F.

2. To peel the onions, bring a large pot of water to a boil. Add the onions and blanch for 1 minute. Remove them with tongs or a slotted spoon and immerse them immediately in ice water to stop the cooking. Drain and peel onions, leaving root intact.

3. Heat oil in a large, deep ovenproof skillet over medium-high heat until almost smoking. Add onions and sauté until they start to brown, about 4 minutes, stirring often. Sprinkle with sugar and salt and pepper to taste and continue to cook until golden brown all over, about 5 more minutes; be careful not to burn the onions.

4. Add vinegar and bring to a boil; boil for about 1 minute. Add orange juice and water to pan. Transfer the pan to oven and braise onions uncovered until onions are cooked through and juices have reduced to a syrupy glaze, about 30 minutes. Be sure to check onions often and add water if liquids have started to boil dry. Garnish with parsley and serve immediately. May be made several hours early and reheated in a 350°F oven until bubbly and hot.

CAPONATA

Sicily is an island of contrasting cultural influences—North African, Middle Eastern, Southern European—and caponata, its signature "salad," is a refection of that cacophony: sweet, salty, crunchy, silky, savory. Every part of the island has its own version of caponata. The combination of vegetables, fruits and nuts brought together with a balm of fragrant olive oil and wine vinegar may shift village to village, but the essence remains raucously Sicilian. I love to serve this as part of a buffet at room temperature, prior to any refrigeration.

¼ cup extra virgin olive oil

1 large unpeeled eggplant, stem removed, cut in bite-size dice

Sea salt and freshly ground black pepper

1 yellow onion, cut in medium dice

2 celery ribs, cut in medium dice

4 plum tomatoes, cored and cut in medium dice

¼ cup red wine vinegar

1½ tablespoons sugar

3 tablespoons golden raisins

⅓ cup pitted green olives, halved lengthwise

3 tablespoons capers in brine, drained

3 tablespoons toasted pine nuts

¼ cup finely chopped flat-leaf parsley

MAKES 4 SERVINGS

1. Heat half of the oil in a large sauté pan over medium heat. Add eggplant, season liberally with salt and pepper and sauté until the eggplant starts to brown and soften, about 5 minutes. Remove from pan and reserve in a bowl.

2. Add more oil if needed and continue to sauté the onion and celery in the same way, separately, removing each vegetable as it is finished to the same bowl with the eggplant.

3. Add everything back into the pan. Add tomatoes and cook until tomatoes give up their liquid and start to break down, about 10 minutes.

4. Add vinegar, sugar, and raisins and simmer uncovered until vegetables are tender, stirring often, about 15 minutes. Add olives, capers, pine nuts and parsley, stirring to combine. Adjust seasoning, allow to cool to room temperature, and serve. May be refrigerated the day before and allowed to come back to room temperature prior to serving or served chilled.

DESSERTS

GRILLED PEACHES WITH HONEY AND YOGURT

Grilling ripe peaches concentrates their flavor, caramelizes their sugar, and adds a whiff of smoke—a far cry from plain old fresh fruit. This quick summer dessert only needs a small dollop of honeyed yogurt to finish it off with elegance. It may be served warm or at room temperature.

1 cup Greek-style yogurt

1 teaspoon honey

½ teaspoon pure vanilla extract

2 tablespoons unsalted butter, melted

4 ripe peaches, halved and pitted

1 teaspoon granulated sugar

  Miniature mint leaves, for garnish

MAKES 4 SERVINGS

1. Mix yogurt, honey and vanilla in a small serving bowl; refrigerate.

2. Preheat grill to medium-high. Brush grill grate with a wire brush and rub the clean grate liberally with oil.

3. Brush peach halves all over with melted butter and sprinkle the cut sides of the fruit with a light coating of sugar. Grill peaches until grill marked, about 2 minutes per side.

4. Serve each peach half with a dollop of yogurt and a garnish of mint. May be served at room temperature.

APPLE CRISP

Crisps, fruit baked under a gilding of sweet streusel crumbs, are the homiest (and easiest) of all baked fruit desserts. This one is classic, and for good reason. It fills the house with the aromatic and fruity scent of apples, cinnamon and butter. I like to serve this crisp warm with a large dollop of crème fraîche.

Butter or spray oil for coating baking pan

8 medium Granny Smith or Golden Delicious apples, peeled, cored and cut in 1-inch thick slices

1 teaspoon ground cinnamon

¼ cup granulated sugar

1 cup firmly packed brown sugar, light or dark

¼ cup plus 2 tablespoons all-purpose flour

1 cup rolled oats

¼ teaspoon fine sea salt

¼ pound (1 stick) cold unsalted butter, cut into small chunks

MAKES 6 SERVINGS

1. Preheat oven to 350°F. Butter a 13 x 9 x 2-inch baking dish or pan; set aside.

2. Combine the apples, cinnamon, granulated sugar, ½ cup of brown sugar, and 2 tablespoons flour in a large mixing bowl. Toss well and pour mixture into the prepared baking dish.

3. Mix remaining flour and brown sugar, the oats, salt and 6 tablespoons of the butter in a medium mixing bowl. Using 2 knives, a pastry blender or your fingers, blend ingredients until they look like coarse crumbs, working quickly to keep butter cold. Scatter this mixture over the apples; dot the top with the remaining butter.

4. Bake until the apples are tender when pierced with a knife and the top is brown and bubbly, about 50 minutes. Put the crisp on a cooling rack to rest for at least 15 minutes before serving. May be served warm or at room temperature.

CRÈME FRAÎCHE

In a pint-size scrupulously clean glass jar, mix 2 tablespoons of the freshest buttermilk or full-fat yogurt and 1 cup pasteurized (not ultrapasteurized) heavy cream. Shake well and set out in a warm place for 12 to 24 hours. I like to put mine in a sunny window. The cream will become thick, tangy and delicious. Store in the fridge, where it will continue to mature and thicken. It keeps for about a week. Makes 1 cup.

PAN-ROASTED APPLES WITH SALTED CARAMEL

Sautéed apples buried beneath a blanket of sweet and salty caramel sauce; it's my version of an adults-only caramel apple. Use tart apples such as Granny Smith to balance the sweetness of the decadent sauce.

¼ pound (1 stick) unsalted butter plus 1 teaspoon for the frying pan

4 Granny Smith or other tart cooking apples, peeled, cored, sliced in half and each half cut into 4 slices

½ cup heavy cream

1 cup granulated sugar

½ cup water

1 teaspoon fleur de sel

MAKES 6 SERVINGS

1. Melt 1 teaspoon butter in a large frying pan over medium heat. Add the apples and sauté until they turn golden and become tender, 5 to 7 minutes. Remove the apples to a serving platter, cover loosely with foil, and set aside.

2. Heat the butter and cream in a small saucepan over medium-low heat just long enough to melt the butter; set aside.

3. Put the sugar in a heavy-bottomed saucepan. Sprinkle the water over the sugar and set over medium heat, allowing the sugar to dissolve. Cook the sugar, watching carefully. As the sugar begins to caramelize, occasionally shake and swirl the pan to evenly distribute the browned sugar. This will take approximately 10 minutes. When the sugar is an even, rich, golden color (be careful, as the mixture can go from pale to burnt very quickly), remove the pan from the heat and carefully add the hot cream and melted butter to the caramel. Stand back; the hot caramel will bubble up the sides of the pan and hot caramel can cause a nasty burn.

4. Return the caramel to low heat, whisking constantly. Cook and stir the caramel for about 2 minutes over the low heat. Remove from the heat and season the sauce with the fleur de sel; stir until it dissolves completely.

5. Drizzle the caramel sauce over the warm apples (or everything in your life) and serve immediately.

RIPE STRAWBERRIES AND VANILLA-SCENTED CREAM

Classics bear repeating, which is why no one tires of fragile-ripe summer sweet strawberries mounded with freshly whipped cream. To perfect this dish, you need do nothing more than seek out a farmstand with freshly picked berries and a local purveyor of plain pasteurized organic cream—no further embellishment is necessary, but I've been known to grate a bit of bittersweet chocolate on top.

1 quart ripe strawberries, rinsed, dried, green tops trimmed, and halved lengthwise

2 tablespoons granulated sugar

1 cup heavy cream

1 teaspoon pure vanilla extract

4 mint springs, for garnish

MAKES 4 SERVINGS

1. Gently toss the strawberries with 1 tablespoon of the sugar in a medium mixing bowl.

2. Combine cream, vanilla and remaining sugar in a chilled medium-large metal mixing bowl. Beat with a hand mixer on high until cream is whipped softly and forms small peaks when the beater is lifted out of the bowl. Do not beat too long or you will wind up with cream that is too stiff.

3. Spoon strawberries into individual bowls and top with a generous dollop of whipped cream. Garnish with mint and serve immediately.

FRENCH COUNTRY CAKE WITH STRAWBERRIES

Simple and simply delicious, this cake is adored by everyone! Perfect for a light dessert, tea time or special breakfast, it is moist, full of fruit and not too sweet. Use the freshest and sweetest strawberries available and gild it with a dollop of freshly whipped cream.

Butter or spray oil and flour for coating baking pan

1 cup sugar, plus 1 tablespoon for topping

¼ pound (1 stick) unsalted butter, softened and cut in 8 chunks

2 large eggs

1 teaspoon pure vanilla extract

1 cup all-purpose flour

1 teaspoon baking powder

Pinch of fine sea salt

1 quart ripe strawberries, rinsed, dried, green tops trimmed, halved lengthwise

MAKES 8 SERVINGS

1. Preheat oven to 350°F. Butter and flour a round 9-inch cake layer pan; set aside.

2. In a stand mixer or with a handheld mixer, cream butter and 1 cup sugar at medium speed until soft and fluffy, about 3 minutes. Beat in eggs thoroughly, one at a time, followed by the vanilla; set aside.

3. Sift flour, baking powder and salt in a separate bowl. Add to the creamed butter mixture, ¼ cup at a time, mixing well after each addition, until combined completely; do not mix longer than necessary. Pour batter into the prepared cake pan.

4. Arrange strawberries in a circular pattern in two rows on the cake batter with the tips pointing towards the rim of the pan. Sprinkle strawberries with remaining tablespoon of sugar and bake until cake is springy and light golden, about 50 minutes. The fruit will sink into the batter.

5. Cool in the pan for 10 minutes on a rack. Carefully run a knife around the side of the cake, unmold onto a plate, and then invert back onto the rack so it is right side up. Allow cake to cool completely and serve at room temperature.

COCONUT RICE PUDDING

I adore coconut. Fresh is best, but I even go for the sweetened processed stuff. Combine that with the best comfort food on earth, rice pudding, and I'm halfway to nirvana. The pungent aroma of fresh nutmeg sets off the creamy custard and the toasted coconut garnish adds lovely crunch—as if it were needed!

3 cups whole milk

1 can (13.5 oz) unsweetened coconut milk

½ cup sugar

½ cup jasmine rice

Pinch of sea salt

1 cup sweetened shredded coconut

Freshly grated nutmeg, for garnish

MAKES 4 SERVINGS

1. Combine milk, coconut milk and sugar in a medium saucepan, stirring until the sugar is moistened. Bring to a simmer over medium heat, stirring often.

2. Stir in the rice and salt. Reduce heat to low and simmer until thickened, stirring often, for 50 minutes to 1 hour. The mixture will seem very loose until the last 5 minutes.

3. Meanwhile, toast 2 tablespoons of the coconut in a dry pan over medium heat, tossing constantly until golden brown. Cool toasted coconut and reserve.

4. Stir the remaining coconut into the finished pudding, cool to room temperature and refrigerate, covered, until well chilled, at least 4 hours.

5. When ready to serve, remove pudding from refrigerator and serve garnished with toasted coconut and nutmeg.

BANANA WALNUT TEA CAKE

There are always ripe bananas in our house and I can't bear to toss them, so banana bread is a common out-the-door breakfast or snack. In an effort to be healthful, I developed this version using whole wheat flour and oatmeal, a grain that keeps breads super moist. Add chocolate chips if you like a richer sweeter version.

Butter or spray oil and flour for coating baking pan

¼ pound (1 stick) unsalted butter, softened and cut in 8 chunks

½ cup granulated sugar

½ cup packed light brown sugar

2 large or extra large eggs, lightly beaten in a small bowl

4 medium very ripe bananas, peeled and mashed

1 cup all-purpose flour

¾ cup whole wheat flour

¾ cup rolled oats

1 teaspoon baking powder

½ teaspoon baking soda

1 teaspoon fine sea salt

1 cup walnut halves and pieces, chopped

½ cup sweetened flaked coconut

1 cup bittersweet chocolate chips (optional)

MAKES 8 SERVINGS

1. Preheat oven to 350°F. Butter and flour a 9 x 3-inch loaf pan; set aside.

2. In a stand mixer or with a handheld mixer, cream butter, sugar and brown sugar at medium speed, until soft and fluffy, about 3 minutes. Beat in eggs and bananas; set aside.

3. Mix the flours, oats, baking powder, baking soda and salt in a separate bowl. Add to the creamed butter mixture; do not mix longer than necessary. Stir in nuts, coconut and chocolate chips (if using). Pour batter into the prepared pan.

4. Bake until a tester inserted into the center comes out with just a crumb or two clinging to it, about 50 minutes.

5. Cool in the pan for 10 minutes on a rack. Carefully run a knife around the side of the cake, unmold onto a plate, and then invert back on to the rack so it is right side up. Allow cake to cool completely and serve warm or at room temperature.

CINNAMON PECAN COFFEE CAKE

This is a wonderful classic coffee cake recipe, swirled with pecans and scented with cinnamon. It was given to me by my stepmother and good friend, Bonnie (she calls herself the "step monster," which she really isn't but makes us laugh). This is a great breakfast or anytime cake. The glaze is optional.

Butter or spray oil and flour for coating baking pan

½ pound (2 sticks) unsalted butter, softened and cut in 8 chunks

1½ cups granulated sugar

3 large or extra large eggs

2 teaspoons pure vanilla extract

2 cups all-purpose flour

1 teaspoon baking powder

¼ teaspoon fine sea salt

1 cup sour cream

½ cup chopped pecans

¼ cup light brown sugar

2 tablespoons cinnamon

½ cup powdered sugar

1 to 2 tablespoons water

¼ teaspoon almond extract

MAKES 10 SERVINGS

1. Preheat oven to 350°F. Butter and flour a 10-inch cake pan or springform pan.

2. In a stand mixer or with a handheld mixer, cream butter and granulated sugar at medium speed until soft and fluffy, about 3 minutes. Beat in eggs thoroughly, one at a time, followed by the vanilla; set aside.

3. Sift flour, baking powder and salt in a separate bowl. Add to the creamed butter mixture in two additions alternating with sour cream. Mix batter on medium speed for 2 minutes.

4. Mix the pecans, brown sugar and cinnamon in a small bowl.

5. Spoon half of the batter into prepared pan. Sprinkle half of the pecan mixture over the batter. Cover with remaining batter. Run a knife through the batter to swirl the filling. Sprinkle remaining pecan mixture over top.

6. Bake until a tester inserted into the center comes out with just a crumb or two clinging to it, about 50 minutes. Cool in the pan on a rack 15 minutes. Carefully run a knife around the side of the cake, unmold onto a plate, and then invert back onto the rack so it is right side up. Allow cake to cool completely.

7. To make the glaze, whisk the powdered sugar, water and almond extract in a small bowl until sooth. Drizzle over the top of the cake.

WARM INDIVIDUAL COCONUT CHOCOLATE CAKES

I adore the texture of flourless chocolate cakes. Not too sweet and densely flavored with chocolate and coconut, this cake never fails to satisfy. I suggest serving it with a dollop of lightly sweetened fresh whipped cream or crème fraîche.

Butter and flour for coating ramekins

4 ounces semisweet chocolate

¼ pound (1 stick) unsalted butter

2 large eggs

2 large egg yolks

¼ cup granulated sugar

2 teaspoon all-purpose flour

2 tablespoon sweetened flaked coconut

Powdered sugar, for garnish

MAKES 4 SERVINGS

1. Preheat oven to 450°F. Butter and lightly flour four 4-ounce ramekins. Tap out the excess flour. Set aside.

2. In the top of a double boiler set over simmering water, heat the butter and chocolate together until the chocolate is almost completely melted.

3. While that's heating, beat the eggs, yolks, and sugar in a medium bowl with a handheld mixer until light and thick. Remove the top of the double boiler from the bottom and slowly beat the egg mixture into the chocolate, then quickly beat in the flour, just until combined. Add coconut and combine with a spatula.

4. Pour the batter into the prepared ramekins and put on a sheet pan. At this point you can refrigerate the desserts until you are ready to eat, for up to several hours; bring them back to room temperature before baking.

5. Bake the cakes on the sheet pan just until the sides set, 6 to 7 minutes; the center will still be soft.

6. Invert each ramekin onto a plate and let sit for about 10 seconds. Unmold by lifting up one edge of the ramekin; the cake will fall out onto the plate. Serve immediately.

RASPBERRY CUSTARD "CAKE"

A cross between custard, pudding and cake, this is a spin on *clafoutis,* the traditional French dessert from Normandy. Typically made with cherries, I've substituted raspberries and added buttermilk for a more delicate texture and a light, tangy flavor. Bake this dessert while you are eating dinner to serve warm, or bake it the night before and refrigerate to serve cold—both options are equally delicious!

Butter for coating baking pan

½ cup sugar plus 2 tablespoons for dusting baking dish

¼ cup whole milk

¼ cup heavy cream

¼ cup buttermilk

3 large eggs

1 teaspoon pure vanilla extract

Pinch of fine sea salt

½ cup all purpose flour

1½ pints ripe red raspberries

Powdered sugar, for garnish

MAKES 6 SERVINGS

1. Preheat oven to 350°F. Butter a 9-inch glass pie plate. Dust with 2 tablespoons sugar, shaking out excess.

2. Blend milk, cream, buttermilk, eggs, sugar, vanilla, salt, and flour in a blender until smooth, about 1 minute, scraping down the sides as needed.

3. Pour half of batter into the prepared pie plate and scatter raspberries on top. Cover with additional batter. Bake until puffy and evenly browned and a knife inserted in the center comes out clean, about 40 minutes.

4. Cool completely in the pan on rack. Carefully run a knife around the side of the cake, unmold onto a plate, and then invert back onto a serving plate so it is right side up. Sprinkle liberally with powdered sugar, or refrigerate and sprinkle with powdered sugar just before serving.

PEACH BROWN SUGAR STREUSEL MUFFINS

This recipe was inspired from a tweet by Ruth Reichl, the former editor of *Gourmet* magazine. Her recipe was for blueberry muffins, but I had fabulous fresh peaches, so I tweaked the recipe and made it my own with outstanding results.

Butter for coating muffin tins

2   cups all-purpose flour

1   cup granulated sugar

2   teaspoons baking powder

1   teaspoon plus a pinch fine sea salt

9   tablespoons unsalted butter, melted

⅓   cup milk

2   large eggs, beaten

2   large peaches, peeled, pitted and cut into large dice

¼   cup packed light brown sugar

¼   teaspoon almond extract

MAKES 12 MUFFINS

1. Preheat oven to 375°F. Butter a standard 12-cup muffin tin; set aside.

2. In a large bowl, sift 1½ cups of the flour, the granulated sugar, baking powder and salt. Stir to mix.

3. Stir in 6 tablespoons of the melted butter, the milk, and eggs into the flour mixture, mixing just enough to combine. Fold in the peaches. Spoon the batter into the buttered muffin tin, filling each cup about halfway.

4. Mix the remaining melted butter, the brown sugar, almond extract, a pinch of salt, and the remaining flour until well combined and crumbly. Sprinkle some over each muffin.

5. Bake until puffed and golden brown, about 20 minutes. Cool in muffin tin for 15 minutes before carefully removing each muffin. Serve warm.

NAKED PUMPKIN PIE

Pumpkin pie was always a favorite harvest-time dessert in our house, and I wanted a way to experience those flavors without the added time (and calories) of pastry. I developed this recipe for a quick "naked" pumpkin pie. I serve it with dollops of crème fraîche flavored with maple syrup.

1   can (15 oz) 100% pure pumpkin

½   cup granulated sugar

¼   cup dark brown sugar

½   teaspoon fine sea salt

1   teaspoon ground cinnamon

1   teaspoon freshly grated gingerroot (use a fine Microplane grater, see page 33)

    Pinch of ground cloves

    Pinch of freshly grated nutmeg

2   large eggs, beaten

½   cup heavy cream

½   cup whole milk

    Softened butter for coating baking dish or ramekins

1   cup crème fraîche, purchased or homemade (page 174)

1   tablespoon real maple syrup

MAKES 6 SERVINGS

1. Preheat oven to 350°F.

2. Mix the pumpkin, sugars, salt and spices in a large mixing bowl with a whisk until smooth. Add eggs, cream, and milk, stirring until smooth.

3. Butter a 1½-quart baking dish or six 4-ounce ramekins. Set in a baking pan and pour boiling water into the pan until it comes half way up the sides of the baking dish or ramekins. Pour the pumpkin mixture into the prepared baking dish(es). Bake just until the filling is set in the center (when you jiggle the dish the mixture will still move a bit), 35 to 40 minutes for ramekins, 50 minutes to 1 hour for a large baking dish.

4. Allow "pie" to cool for at least 2 hours and serve or refrigerate for serving the next day.

5. Garnish with crème fraîche mixed with maple syrup.

CHOCOLATE ORANGE FAUX POTS DE CRÈME

This is clearly the most ridiculously simple, drop-dead decadent chocolate desserts of all time. It can be prepared in five minutes (plus refrigeration time) and served in decorative glasses for entertaining or as an everyday treat during the week. The mixture is so rich you only need a few bites.

1   cup half-and-half

6   ounces bittersweet chocolate chunks or chips

2   large or extra large eggs at room temperature

2   tablespoons orange liqueur, such as Grand Marnier or Cointreau

    Pinch fine of sea salt

    Crème fraîche, purchased or homemade (page 174), for garnish

    Finely shredded orange zest, for garnish

MAKES 6 SERVINGS

1. Scald the half and half in a small saucepan just until bubbles form at the edge of the liquid; do not boil.

2. Meanwhile, blend the chocolate, eggs, orange liqueur, and salt In a blender on high for about 1 minute. Carefully add the hot cream through the removable cap in the lid of the blender. Continue to blend the mixture on high for another 30 to 60 seconds, until the mixture is completely smooth, scraping the sides down, as needed. Allow to rest for 5 minutes.

3. Pour and scrape into serving glasses and chill in the refrigerator until set, at least 3 hours or overnight.

4. Garnish each pot with a dollop of crème fraîche or a curled strip of orange zest.

EQUIVALENCY TABLE

VOLUME	MEASURE		OVEN TEMPERATURE	
U.S.	Metric		°F	°C
¼ tsp	1.25 ml		250	120
½ tsp	2.5 ml		275	140
1 tsp	5 ml		300	150
1 Tbsp (3 tsp)	15 ml		325	160
1 fl oz (2 Tbsp)	30 ml		350	180
¼ cup (4 Tbsp)	60 ml		375	190
⅓ cup	80 ml		400	200
½ cup	120 ml		425	220
1 cup	240 ml		450	230
1 pint (2 cups)	480 ml		475	240
1 quart (4 cups)	960 ml		500	260
2 quarts	1.92 l			
1 gallon (4 quarts)	3.84 l			

WEIGHT	MEASURE
1 oz	28 g
1 lb	448 g
2.2 lb	1 kg

INDEX